W9-CJE-611

Country
Confidential

Get the lowdown on:

The dirt-poor days

"Back home, when you got cold the best you could do to keep warm was to throw another hound dog in the bed. And if you didn't have a hound dog, you got married."
(Tennessee Ernie Ford)

Bad-hair days

"I have to keep washing and blow-drying it. If it gets too high, I start to look like an evangelist."
(Bryan White)

Lonely days

"I don't gamble or go to bars . . . and I've got lots of time to, like, find a man or whatever."
(Lila McCann)

Fun-filled days

"I'm sure older guys are great lovers. But I just happen to like young guys."
(Dottie West)

Really bad days

"They put me in a straitjacket in the driveway of my dream home. Thank God the authorities didn't come on a concert day. No telling how many fans would have seen."
(George Jones, about the day he allegedly shot at wife Tammy Wynette)

and

Last days

"No matter how big you get, the size of your funeral depends on the weather."
(Roger Miller)

Coral Amende is the author/editor of the gossip-studded crossword puzzle in *Los Angeles* magazine and the author of *Hollywood Confidential: An Inside Look at the Public Careers and Private Lives of Hollywood's Rich and Famous* (available in a Plume edition). She doesn't live anywhere near Nashville.

TECHNICAL COLLEGE OF THE LOWCOUNTRY
LEARNING RESOURCES CENTER
POST OFFICE BOX 1288
BEAUFORT SOUTH CAROLINA 29901-1288

Also by Coral Amende

*Hollywood Confidential: An Inside Look at the Public Careers and Private
Lives of Hollywood's Rich and Famous*

Random House Famous Name Finder

If You Don't Have Anything Nice to Say . . . Come Sit Next to Me

. The RPG Game Collection

TECHNICAL COLLEGE OF THE LOWCOUNTRY
LEARNING RESOURCES CENTER
POST OFFICE BOX 1288
BEAUFORT, SOUTH CAROLINA 29901-1288

TECHNICAL COLLEGE OF THE LOWCOUNTRY
LEARNING RESOURCES CENTER
POST OFFICE BOX 1288
BEAUFORT, SOUTH CAROLINA 29901-1288

Country Confidential

**The Lowdown
on the
High Living,
Heartbreaking,
and Hell-Raising
of Country Music's
Biggest Stars**

CORAL AMENDE

A PLUME BOOK

TECHNICAL COLLEGE OF THE LOWCOUNTRY
LEARNING RESOURCES CENTER
POST OFFICE BOX 1288
BEAUFORT, SOUTH CAROLINA 29901-1288

PLUME
Published by the Penguin Group
Penguin Putnam Inc., 375 Hudson Street, New York, New York 10014, U.S.A.
Penguin Books Ltd, 27 Wrights Lane, London W8 5TZ, England
Penguin Books Australia Ltd, Ringwood, Victoria, Australia
Penguin Books Canada Ltd, 10 Alcorn Avenue, Toronto, Ontario, Canada M4V 3B2
Penguin Books (N.Z.) Ltd, 182–190 Wairau Road, Auckland 10, New Zealand

Penguin Books Ltd, Registered Offices: Harmondsworth, Middlesex, England

First published by Plume, a member of Penguin Putnam Inc.

First Printing, November, 1999
1 3 5 7 9 10 8 6 4 2

Copyright © Coral Amende, 1999
All rights reserved

Ⓡ REGISTERED TRADEMARK—MARCA REGISTRADA

LIBRARY OF CONGRESS CATALOGING-IN-PUBLICATION DATA
Amende, Coral.
    Country confidential : the lowdown on the high living, heart-
breaking, and hell-raising of country music's biggest stars / by
Coral Amende.
        p.   cm.
    Includes index.
    ISBN 0-452-28119-9
    1. Country music—history and criticism. 2. Country musicians.
ML3524.A54 1999   99-24341
781.642'0973—dc21   CIP

Printed in the United States of America
Set in Americana
Designed by Coral Amende

Without limiting the rights under copyright reserved above, no part of this publication
may be reproduced, stored in or introduced into a retrieval system, or transmitted, in
any form, or by any means (electronic, mechanical, photocopying, recording, or
otherwise), without the prior written permission of both the copyright owner and the
above publisher of this book.

BOOKS ARE AVAILABLE AT QUANTITY DISCOUNTS WHEN USED TO PROMOTE PRODUCTS OR SERVICES.
FOR INFORMATION PLEASE WRITE TO PREMIUM MARKETING DIVISION, PENGUIN PUTNAM INC.,
375 HUDSON STREET, NEW YORK, NEW YORK 10014.

The following page constitutes an extension of this copyright page.

Line art courtesy of:
Art Parts
Corel Corporation
Havana Street
T/Maker Company

Courtesy of **Star File Photo Agency, Inc.**:
Trisha Yearwood (page 2): Chuck Pulin
Mindy McCready (page 34): Jeffrey Mayer
Alan Jackson (page 37): David Seelig
Shania Twain (page 39): Vinnie Zuffante
Tanya Tucker (page 42): Dominick Conde
Tanya Tucker (page 43): Jeffrey Mayer
Dolly Parton (page 45): Brett Lee
Kenny Rogers (page 48): Larry Kaplan
Loretta Lynn (page 50): John Lee
Clint Black (page 70): Chuck Pulin
Billy Ray Cyrus (page 78): Jana
Mindy McCready (page 81): Debra Shade
Garth Brooks (page 105): Chuck Pulin
Garth Brooks (page 118): Chuck Pulin
LeAnn Rimes (page 137): Jeffrey Mayer
Tanya Tucker and Howie Mandel (page 153):
Dominick Conde
Tammy Wynette (page 157): Chuck Pulin
Randy Travis and Lib Hatcher (page 161):
Mike Guastella
Willie Nelson and Waylon Jennings (pages
164–165): Chuck Pulin
Dottie West and Mark Miller (page 175): Brian
Stern
Tracy Lawrence and Stacie Drew (page 179):
Jeffrey Mayer
Hank Williams, Jr. (page 205): Vinnie Zuffante
Merle Haggard (page 213): John Lee
Johnny Paycheck and Kinky Friedman
(pages 218–219): Chuck Pulin

CONTENTS

The Roots of My Raisin'

1

 Rags to Rhinestones

2

Gone Country

3

CONTENTS

4

Talk of the Town

🎺〰️🎺〰️🎺 Cashville, Tennessee 🎺〰️🎺〰️🎺

5

They Don't Make Love Like They Used To

6

Sturm und Twang

7

➤~➤~◀ I Fall to Pieces ➤~➤~

8

1

The Roots of My Raisin'

"If you think country is still about big hair and blue eye shadow, you haven't listened to it for twenty years—and you probably think that Elton John is still wearing platforms."
(Trisha Yearwood)

COUNTRY MUSIC

Used to be you'd hear those two words and several things sprang immediately to mind: singing through the nose, twangy gee-tars, and wailin' fiddles; tear-in-your-beer tunes about mama, Jesus, and faithless spouses; *Hee Haw*, hay bales, and hoedowns; not-of-this-earth hairstyles, high as the Himalayas and sculpted into gravity-defying mounds of mondo-whip dessert topping; ruffled, puffy-sleeved, big-skirted dresses (heavy on the sequins, please), spangled Nudie suits, big ol' jewelry, and high-heeled boots; and guitar-shaped swimming pools and gold-plated Cadillacs.

My, how the times have a-changed. Country has graduated from a geographically limited genre into a full-fledged phenomenon rivaling the popularity of pop music, and its stars are now craftily marketed products of the same big-business music machine as their more mainstream counterparts. It's getting harder all the time to tell the difference between country and straight-ahead adult contemporary. Canny careerist **Trisha Yearwood**'s stops-out "How Do I Live Without You" has none of the hallmarks of a traditional hillbilly hit, nor do shockingly tiny-eyed **LeAnn Rimes**'s bombastic ballads of terminally grandiose "inspiration" or rock-chick-wannabe **Shania Twain**'s sexually charged come-ons—in fact, the only way you can tell country songs from pop tunes these days is by a slight drawl and perhaps a token steel-guitar lick somewhere in the solo. The "honk" style of singing has been almost completely purged, replaced by layer upon layer of harmony and slick studio production that wouldn't be out of place in the latest overblown Celine Dion or Mariah Carey record.

Despite country's new "class," its stars, whether established or new, young or superannuated, remain true to the old-school values that made country great: God, home, and family; lyin' and cheatin'; fightin' and feudin'; gettin' hitched and gettin' divorced; and, of course, drinkin', druggin', and raisin' hell.

Lifestyles of the Not So Rich and Famous

"I'm as country as they come. I was born on a farm with no indoor plumbing or electricity, and I plowed behind a mule."
(Razzy Bailey)

Tales of hardship during one's raisin' used to be as common as corn bread. But today's crop of country stars, who grew up amid strip malls and fast-food joints rather than hard-packed fields and broken-down barns, have had it easy— especially when you compare them to the hillbilly heroes of yesteryear. Back then, it almost used to be re-

quired that one had to have had a terribly arduous upbringing, full of sweat-of-the-brow labor and deprivation. **Bobby Bare**'s family was so tapped out that they were forced to give up his young sister for adoption. **Roger Miller**, who went on to find fame and fortune as one of Nashville's cleverest tune-crafters, suffered simi- larly: "My father died when I was a year old," he recalled. "There were three little boys— I was the youngest—and my mother couldn't support us, so she was going to put us in an orphanage. My father had three brothers and one lived in Arkansas, one in Oklahoma, and one in California. Each came and took a boy home and raised him. I went to Oklahoma." (Specifi- cally to Erick, which, according to Miller, was "so small that the city limits signs are back to back. Its population is fifteen hundred including rakes and tractors.")

> "I spent the early part of my life looking at the north end of a southbound mule, and it didn't take long to figure out that a guitar was a lot lighter than a plow handle."
> **(Glen Campbell)**

Many of the future famous spent lots of time in "high cotton"—not exactly living in style, but toilin' in the fields, pickin' the durn stuff. As a young whippersnapper, **Charley Pride** earned a whopping three bucks for every hundred pounds he harvested, and **Johnny Cash** was draggin' a nine-foot sack by the time he was twelve. **Tammy Wynette**, who could haul in an impressive two hundred pounds a day, hated it with a passion and said that "the only thing that got me through was daydreaming." Same for **Willie Nelson**, who recalls, "I didn't like picking cotton one bit. I used to stand in the fields and watch the cars go by and think, 'I want to go with them.'"

> "When I was little, my sister and I used to go down to the pasture and bring the cows in for milking. And when it was the fall, we'd go out and help with the harvest, fix lunch, and take it down to the people working. That's how it is, and you don't think about it."
> **(Martina McBride)**

Glen Campbell, who weeps, wails, and beats his breast as if he's suffered more than anyone in the history of country music, also worked up a sweat in the cotton fields and had to share a bunk with three brothers. The big highlight of the week would come with the broadcast of the Grand Ole Opry—whenever his poverty-stricken parents could scare up a few pennies for radio

batteries, that is. "On the survival scale," he whimpers, "my family was just a step above the animals that we ate to stay alive." He bravely remembers with a wistful fondness the days back when, "I had dropped out of school and left my home. I was living the stories about which country songs are written." Things ultimately turned around for the bulbous-nosed young boy, though: "When I was a kid, my family didn't have electric lights. I eventually would see my name glowing in electric letters taller than some of the houses in which I was raised." Oh, the drama.

Bobbie Gentry was raised by her grandparents in a tumbledown shack with no plumbing or electricity. (Her surrogate parents were good to her, though—when they noticed the little girl's musical talent, they swapped one of their cows for a piano so she'd have something to play.) **Tennessee Ernie Ford** remembered his raisin' in primitive surroundings: "Back home, when you got cold the best you could do to keep warm was to throw another hound dog in the bed. And if you didn't have a hound dog, you got married." (So *that* explains **Loretta Lynn**'s and **Tammy Wynette**'s choice of husbands.)

Coal Miners' Daughters

The saga of **Loretta Lynn**'s early years has been immortalized in everything from songs to books to movies, and it goes something like this: she grew up in Kentucky, in the quaintly named Butcher Hollow (or "Holler," as Loretta tells it); married at thirteen; became a mother soon after (in fact she had four kids before she was old enough to drink!); lived in a shack with no running water; and so on and so forth. (In fact, **Crystal Gayle**, Loretta's more glamorous sister, was the only one of the large brood who was born in a hospital.) Fellow Kentuckian **Patty Loveless** had a similar raisin': she's from the quaintly named Belcher Holler and is also the daughter of a coal miner (sadly, her dad died of black lung). Liftin' yourself up out of miserable circumstances is a hallmark of any good country career, and both of these hard-luck ladies have done just that, rising to the top of the hillbilly heap in the process.

I'm the Only Hell My Mama Ever Raised

Speaking of miserable milieus, **Merle Haggard**'s family, victims of the Depression, lived in an old railroad refrigerator car when he was a tot, and his daddy died when li'l Merle was just nine years old—a factor that was most likely at the root of the Hag's early descent into a life of juvenile delinquency, frequent arrests, and hard time in the hoosegow.

Billy Dean got into some trouble as a youngster too, albeit with less drastic consequences than Merle. While playing with matches as a little kid, he burned down the ol' homestead. Okay, one mistake is allowed. But this was followed a few years later by his shooting the family gas station full of holes while emulating TV's *Rifleman*, Chuck Connors. Somebody shove some Ritalin down that kid's throat!

"I was just a real curious kid. I wasn't really destructive or anything."
(Billy Dean)
Obviously.

There will never be a shortage of heart-wrenching country songs about hard working, blue-collar daddies and saintly, self-sacrificing mamas. But it wasn't that way for everybody. **Sammy Kershaw** remembers his pa with something less than unmitigated fondness: "Three beers and he was a crazy man. . . . We used to be punished with rice. You ever try to kneel on rice for an hour? It doesn't seem like much, but it sure hurts."

Tim McGraw didn't even know who his father was until his mom revealed her secret (after eleven-year-old Tim's snooping turned up his birth certificate). Turns out that Tim was the product of a summertime fling between mom and pro baseball player Tug McGraw. Tim and Tug struck up a relationship and continue to keep in touch, and Tug, now in his late seventies, recently blessed Tim with a new half brother!

Child Support

Little **Chet Atkins** made his first gee-tar out of a ukulele and some old screen wire. But, he remembers, he "didn't have it that long. I was plunking on it one day when my mother asked me to go to the spring to get some water. I didn't go quick enough, so she took it out of my hands and hit me over the head with it and broke the neck off."

"There's no greater compliment you can give your parents than to say you want to be just like them."
(Barbara Mandrell)

Belly button–bejeweled **Mindy McCready** had a somewhat vivacious, very flirtatious wannabe beauty queen mother who, after divorcing Mindy's dad, began hitting the singles bars—with young Mindy, dolled up in Mom's duds and makeup, in tow (cheaper than a baby-sitter). When Mom split up with a man she'd mistaken for Mr. Right, she decided to get revenge by sending her daughter to break into his house and grab everything of value—which sixteen-year-old Mindy dutifully did. It's worth noting that Mindy's mom takes all the credit for "creating" her famous daughter—a claim that seems more than justified considering Mindy's romantic track record.

Po' Folks

SO JUST HOW POOR WERE YE?

"Poor, real poor."
(**Kenny Rogers**, whose family lived in a housing project)

"I was born poor and raised poor."
(**Spade Cooley**)

"I'm just a 'billy from the hills where the land is so poor you've got to put fertilizer around the telephone poles before you can speak."
(**Uncle Dave Macon**)

"We were so poor that our outhouse was the woods."
(Alabama's **Teddy Gentry**)

"Oh, I was a hardworkin' little boy. Pullin' cotton, shockin' grain, cuttin' wheat, loadin' wheat, choppin' cotton, cleanin' chicken houses, milkin' cows, plowin'. They used to laugh at my clothes, my bib overalls and galluses, because we were dirt poor."
(**Jimmy Dean**, the sausage king)

"Mama would say, 'Kids, pour more water in the soup. Better days are coming.'"
(Ashley Judd)

"When you grow up poor, like I did, you have to try and look at the light side of it. Not that being poor is all hoots and giggles—but if you look at it the right way, there's bound to have been some funny moments."
(Mark Miller)

"We were so poor you'd have to spell it with five o's."
(Roger Miller)

"We never actually starved, but sometimes we never had quite enough to eat."
(Dolly Parton, who dined on rock-flavored soup as a kid, and still slumbers with a night-light on because of the rodents that used to scuttle about in her bedroom)

"I grew up in Georgia. We weren't starvin' poor or anything, but we weren't that well-off. We grew up more backwards than we did poor."
(Alan Jackson, who slept in a hallway for years because he didn't have his own bed)

"I was brought up where you squeezed a penny so hard Lincoln blinks."
(Vern Gosdin)

The Girl Most Likely

Shania Twain was raised in Timmins, Ontario, by her mother and her stepfather, Jerry Twain. Twain, an Ojibwa Indian, adopted little Shania, and when her star began to rise, she returned the favor— by claiming to be half Ojibwa (and changing her name from Eileen to Shania, which means "I'm on my way" in Ojibwa), at least until journalists uncovered this romanticized half-truth about her life (the brouhaha was started by a Timmins newspaper, which ceased writing about their native daughter after she threatened to sue). Shania's well-publicized accounts of her impoverished youth have also raised a few eyebrows. Her tales of her early life include descriptions of Timmins—a thriving metropolis— as a jerkwater roadstop where you had to catch your own food if you wanted to eat, along with dramatic accounts of subsisting on nothing but mustard sandwiches and a bread, milk, and sugar stew (see below)—although she also claimed her family never had milk to drink with their potatoes. (Maybe they shouldn't have used it all with their stew, then.)

Mark Twain's Words

Shania Speaks Out About Her Underprivileged Youth

"We were extremely poor when I was a kid, and my mother was often depressed—with five children and no food to feed them."

"We were hungry a lot when we were kids."

"I'd judge other kids' wealth by their lunches. If a kid had baked goods, that was like, oh, they must be rich."

"We would go for days with just bread and milk and sugar, and heat it up in a pot."

"I still bathe with a cup."

Family Tradition

"Nobody likes the kids of famous people.
It's particularly hard if you go into the
profession where the parent has been
very successful. But if that's where your
talents lie, it's dumb not to pursue it.
Doctors' children become doctors. It
shouldn't be all that strange that Johnny
Cash's child likes to sing."
(Rosanne Cash)

Country Value Number One is God, of course—followed closely by Family. And country music, like most other show businesses, has a history of favoring the genetically blessed. A few of the industry's closer family ties:

Rosanne Cash is the daughter of **Johnny**, who is married to **June Carter Cash**, who is the mother of **Carlene Carter**, whose grandmother is **Maybelle Carter**. Carlene is **Rosanne Cash**'s stepsister, and they both dated **Rodney Crowell** (Rosanne also married him). **Cindy Cash**, Rosanne's sister, wed **Marty Stuart**, and Carlene was hitched to **Jack Ruth**, who later wed Cindy. Are you with me?

Shelly West is **Dottie**'s daughter, but was never quite as successful as her ultra-extroverted mom.

Deana Carter's doting dad, **Fred Carter, Jr.**, was a well-known Nashville guitarist.

Lorrie Morgan's proud papa, **George**, had a hit with "Candy Kisses" in the fifties and was a longtime Grand Ole Opry performer.

Pam Tillis is **Mel**'s daughter.

Matraca Berg is the daughter of singer/songwriter **Icee Berg**, who was married to songwriter/guitarist **Dave Kirby**. She's also **Patsy Cline**'s third cousin.

Crystal Gayle is **Loretta Lynn**'s sister. What's the big diff between the two stellar sibs? Sneers Crystal, "I've learned from her mistakes. She never knows ahead of time what she's doing. When the time comes, she's told. I'm more my own boss."

Naomi and Wynonna Judd are the best-selling mother-daughter combo Nashville has yet produced. "Wynonna and I began singing together, frankly, because there were times when we wouldn't talk to each other," admits Naomi. Wy seconds that emotion: "We are not the Brady Bunch. We put the fun in dysfunctional." Naomi adds, "It's more like *The Agony and the Ecstasy*." In fact, the dueling duo have been known to resort to physical violence when they really get pushed out of shape—one particularly nasty quarrel resulted in bruises, scrapes, bloodied fingernails, and a damaged car (Naomi got into hers and ran into Wy's).

Garth's (whaddaya mean, Garth who?) mom, **Colleen Carroll**, was in the biz—she recorded for Capitol and performed with **Red Foley**. And GB's dad? A pretty pragmatic individual, apparently. Says sonny boy, "We were in Tulsa [before Garth's big Central Park concert wingding], and I told Dad, 'There could be half a million people in Central Park.' I was saying it like, 'Aren't you impressed, Dad?' And Dad's response was, 'You know, that's half a million people you could disappoint.' So my dad is a very real guy."

Hank Williams, Jr. undoubtedly got noticed because of his legendary pa. But, he snarls, "I got so fuckin' sick of hearin' people say, 'Oh God, your poor ole daddy, he wasn't treated right. He was the king and we loved him.' Well, they *hated* Daddy in Nashville."

Grandpa Told Me So

Besides teaching their children good manners and old-fashioned values, the parents and grandparents of some of country's brightest stars also made sure to give them some *really good advice.*

"Mama always told me, 'Nobody's going to put the dime in the phone for you, Melvin. You've got to do it yourself.'"
(Mel Tillis)

"After my arrest, I worried about my ability to be a role model. My grandmother told me, 'I don't know of any role model who started out as Snow White.'"
(Ty Herndon)

"My father said, 'Know where you're going, always be aware of where you're at, and, most of all, never forget where you come from.'"
(Billy Ray Cyrus)

"My grandmother always said, 'The best thing for the inside of a kid is the outside of a horse.'"
(Lynn Anderson)

"[My grandmother] said, 'While we're here on this earth we strive to get out of the dirt. If you think this is all you're ever going to amount to, then you go on and play in the dirt all you want. But if you let somebody else tell you what to do with your life, then I don't know what to think.'"
(Ty Herndon)

"My dad always told me the more you stomp in crap the worse it stinks."
(Billy Ray Cyrus)

". . . with Mom's encouragement I devoured English. She'd say, 'Words are the clothes our thoughts wear, and I know you love to be well dressed!'"
(Wynonna)

Learning As You Go

> "I got so involved in music, and that's when I started screwing up in school. . . . Now I wish I had stayed in school, 'cause I missed out on all the fun, all the things that teenagers experience."
> **(Mark Chesnutt)**

Far from the uneducated, back-woods yokels who first populated country's charts and stages, today's suburban cowboys and cowgirls are proud possessors of college degrees and are less likely to have gone through the school of hard knocks than the school of hard rock—witness megalomaniacal megastar **Garth Brooks**, who cites KISS, Journey, and Styx as a few of his influences.

More than any other performer, Garth (or "GB," as he refers to himself) typifies the new breed of calculated country celebs, who plot their every maneuver with the planning and precision of a major military campaign. Brooks, the best-selling country artist of all time, majored in marketing at the University of Oklahoma, "in the middle of average Oklahoma, in the middle of average America," he says modestly. ("Sure ain't the way I did it," snaps **Reba McEntire**.) It's an education he's putting to good use in the music business, where this "800-pound hillbilly gorilla" (as his ex-boss, axed Liberty Records head **Jimmy Bowen**, calls him) wields a big enough stick to have key record-company executives fired because he doesn't like them (see page 115). Ride 'em, cowboy!

Lyle Lovett earned college degrees in both journalism and German, Ivy Leaguer **Mary Chapin Carpenter** studied American Civ, **Dwight Yoakam** majored in history and philosophy, and **Reba** got into classical music (how clearly can you hear *that* influence in her music?). Spouse-of-Faith **Tim McGraw** wanted to be a lawyer but, he sighs, "I got my grades back the first semester and I knew *that* wasn't going to work." Well, the legal profession's loss is country music's gain—otherwise we wouldn't have that brilliant "Indian Outlaw" record.

But in days of yore, many hard-workin' youngsters just didn't have the *time* for no schoolin'. **Stoney Edwards** remembers the hardscrabble days of his mis-spent youth: "Runnin' corn liquor and helpin' to take care of [my brothers and sisters], I was only able to go up to the third grade. Later, I was too old. I was plum 'shamed to go back to school. I still don't know how to read and write."

Marty Stuart recalls having "a school-teacher who told me I could make something out of myself if I would get my mind off music and get it on to history. I told her that I was more into making history than learning about it." (If nothing else, svelte Stuart will make history for wearing the tightest jeans in Music City.) And **Willie Nelson** remembers being "asked to either stop playin' honky-tonks or drop my Sunday school class. Since Sunday school wasn't payin' me as much as the beer joints, I had to leave the church." Sometimes you've just gotta make the tough calls.

School Daze

Country's High School Dropouts

Glen Campbell
Mark Chesnutt
Freddy Fender
Merle Haggard
Waylon Jennings
Loretta Lynn
Randy Travis

Lucinda Williams was once expelled from elementary school for refusing to salute the flag!

Little Miss Honky-Tonk

"I'm very involved in the business part of my career. That's one thing I don't stay out of. I want to know what's going on, because it's my life."
(LeAnn Rimes)

Country has a history of producing talented tots who accomplish major milestones before they've even hit puberty. The most famous (in recent memory, anyway) is singularly single-minded **LeAnn Rimes**. From the very beginning, she knew she wanted to be a star—"It's always been [her] idea", says her mother, Belinda—and she pursued her goal with eyes-on-the-prize ambition since she was little more than a toddler. Where did all this drive come from? Well, Mom feels it might be the result of divine intervention. "When Wilbur and I married, I was eighteen," she explains. "Everyone else was having babies right off. But we never had a child. I thought we never might. I started praying. A few months later, I became pregnant with LeAnn. That's when I knew God had plans for LeAnn, that his will had touched her heart. . . . I pray every day for her to remain humble. And that she never forgets where her voice comes from."

Then the little country singer asked, "Grandma, why do you wear your hair so big?" "The better to

Lately, the young Renaissance woman has turned her precociously prodigious talents to other avocations, like acting and writing books. An *Entertainment Weekly* review of her saccharine *Holiday in Your Heart* novel (its protagonist is, of all things, a very young, aspiring country diva named Anna Lee—get it?), included this choice sentiment: "As Anna Lee toys with choosing fame over family, an unnamed, huge-haired, legendary country singer tells her a corker of a cautionary tale. Anna Lee says at the finale, 'I felt like I'd been hit over the head with a hammer.' She's not the only one."

Other prepubescent prodigies:

☀ *Age 4*: **Razzy Bailey** made his first record (for an Arkansas five-and-dime); **Patsy Cline** won an amateur tap-dancing contest.

☀ *Age 5*: **Ricky Skaggs** had already mastered the mandolin. By the time he was ten, he could play just about anything you threw at him—and so well that he won a spot on **Flatt and Scruggs**'s Nashville TV show. There was a downside to being a prodigy, though. As Ricky remembers, "I never got to play any sports like football or baseball. My father was afraid something bad would happen to my hands."

☀ *Age 6*: "I guess when I was about six, I sang with **[Bob Wills]** on a radio show." **(Lee Roy Parnell)**

☀ *Age 8*: **Spade Cooley** played his first paying gig.

☀ *Age 11*: **Babs Mandrell** was a regular on *Town Hall Party*, a Southern California TV show. The very next year, she made her network debut on *Five Star Jubilee*.

☀ *Age 12*: **Waylon Jennings** had his own show on a Texas radio station; **David Houston** appeared on *The Louisiana Hayride*.

☀ *Age 13*: **Dolly Parton** released her first single, "Puppy Love." A *Billboard* reviewer, unaware of her age, complained that she sounded like she was twelve.

Kritics' Korner

✮ LeAnn Rimes ✮

"... sounds like Celine Dion in training."
(USA Today)

"... ruining her reputation by flooding the marketplace with albums, videos, and TV specials. ..."
(Star Tribune)

"... belts out the songs ... like a naïve talent-show queen."
(People)

"... inane recording and TV projects. ..."
(St. Louis Post-Dispatch)

"... [*Holiday in Your Heart* is] one of the worst TV movies ever made. [It is] sappy and sentimental and poorly acted and hokey and predictable and boring and laughable."
(Dallas Morning News)

I'm Just an Old Chunk of Coal (But I'm Gonna Be a Diamond Someday)

"I was totally enamored with *The Wizard of Oz.* I always wanted to lean against a haystack and sing."
(Lari White)

The road to success is always a long, hard one, but you've gotta start someplace—and that place is oftentimes the closest: home sweet home. "At family reunions you either found a harmony part or washed dishes, so I chose the harmony part," **Deana Carter** says about the start of her stellar singing career. **Chely Wright** had a good time at her family get-togethers, too: "Everybody played an instrument. Everyone sings—but none of 'em are crazy enough to do it for a living except me!" **Faith Hill** first performed in front of family members when her mama "started paying me twenty-five cents to sing for relatives at reunions. If it was a big family reunion, it went up to fifty cents." Wahoo! But little **Patty Loveless** would only croon on cue if she could go into another room where she wouldn't be seen.

"I was just a little girl when my sister would hold a flashlight and shine it on me like a spotlight so I could put on shows for the family in the living room."
(Lorrie Morgan)

The Bellamy Brothers' (Howard and David) dad booked their first paid gig at a rustic rattle-snake roundup, and **Tanya Tucker**'s papa supposedly won enough playing keno (it must have taken a loooooong time) to finance a demo for his darling daughter, who went on to have a number-one record ("Delta Dawn") at age thirteen. Tucker, a hamolina since birth, needed no prodding to take that ball and run with it—in fact, she'd already made more than a few of her own breaks. When she was just nine, the brassy lass accosted **Mel Tillis** at a county fair and spat out her lofty ambition in no uncertain terms: "'Well, I'm a singer and I want to get started.' He listened to me blurt one out and said, 'My God!'" She walked onstage with him that very night (and no, she didn't flash the audience). Some young per-formers need a bit more encouragement than that, though: teen queen **Lila McCann** once had to be coaxed out of her dressing room with the promise of a new Barbie doll, which her parents agreed to buy for her on one condition: She had to finish her song in enough time that they could get there before the store closed.

> "I wasn't in a band or anything cool like that. I just hogged the karaoke mic. I went to Nashville and brought my karaoke tapes with me."
> (Mindy McCready)

Young 'n' lukewarmily hunky **James Bonamy** got some rather left-handed en-couragement at the start of his journey to success: "People would say, 'You know, you should pursue [country music]. You're not that bad. . . . You're not that good, but you're not that bad!'" **Ty Herndon**, too, remem-bers hearin' a couple of times that he wouldn't amount to a puddle of warm spit: One complaint was, "You sound like a million other people."

Herndon remembers, "I'd been rejected and had so many doors slammed into my face, it got to where it was hard to keep believing in myself. One guy went so far as to tell me, 'Son, you go on back to Alabama, get on your little red tractor, and stay there.'" And luckily for us, virtuoso **Vince Gill** didn't take it to heart when he and his band were booed off the stage while opening a show for KISS during the hard rockers' heyday in the '70s. (Mmm yes, bluegrass and heavy metal—let's do that more often.)

Eddie Rabbitt got his big break at Boy Scout camp. "They had a talent contest," he reminisced, "so I played the two chords I knew on the guitar, sang 'Rock-a-Baby,' and won. For winning, I got a basket-weaving kit, a big leather belt, ten Clark bars, and the satisfaction of knowing *I had arrived*."

It takes a lot of staying power to outlast all the hard knocks spotlight-seekers are bound to endure on their long journey to the top of the hillbilly heap. Fearless **Patsy Cline** bunked on park benches when she first blew in to Nashville. **Johnny Rodriguez** remembers, "I only had about four pairs of pants and three shirts and a guitar. I was livin' out of the trunk of my car, literally." **David Lee Murphy** crashed in a tent in a buddy's backyard for a few months while he was struggling to make it, and things got so desperate for fledgling performer **Willie Nelson** that he offered to sell his song "Hello Walls" to big star **Faron Young** for five hundred bucks. Faron gave him the dough, but magnanimously let him keep the ditty—a good thing for Willie, because it went on to earn a fortune. (In later years, Young complained that Nelson had never repaid the loan; Willie insisted that Faron had refused payback every time he'd offered.)

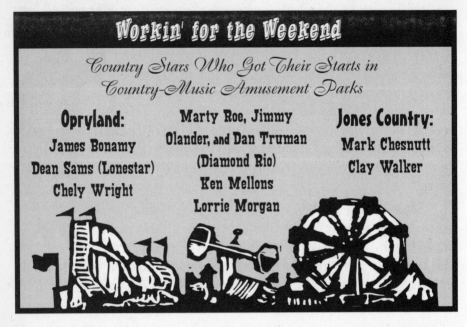

Workin' for the Weekend

Country Stars Who Got Their Starts in Country-Music Amusement Parks

Opryland:

James Bonamy

Dean Sams (Lonestar)

Chely Wright

Marty Roe, Jimmy Olander, and Dan Truman (Diamond Rio)

Ken Mellons

Lorrie Morgan

Jones Country:

Mark Chesnutt

Clay Walker

The Nashville area's theme parks can be a good place to hone your chops and get noticed. **Suzy Bogguss** began her performing career at Dollywood in nearby Pigeon Forge (she also used to book travel posing as her own personal secretary in an attempt to come off as a true professional). **John Anderson** tried out for a gig at Opryland, but apparently his star quality wasn't blindingly evident at the time—he didn't get in because he couldn't hack the audition. **LeAnn Rimes**, **Sawyer Brown**, **Ty Herndon**, and **James Bonamy**'s professional profiles were heightened by appearances on *Star Search*, on which **John Berry** appeared as well (bummer, though—he got his butt whupped by an insurance adjuster). Berry also signed up for a Marlboro talent contest but lost to **Ronnie Dunn**, who soon after hooked up with fellow hopeful **Kix Brooks** to form the most successful country duo ever.

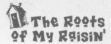
Kris Kristofferson decided to take matters into his own mitts when he convinced himself he'd written a hit. Kristofferson, a former military pilot, was laboring as a janitor at the studio in which **Johnny Cash** recorded. (Kris made a point of toiling in Johnny's room every time the star was in residence, according to Cash, who remembers him "carrying out trash at two in the morning.") Unfortunately, he was forbidden to pitch songs on the job under threat of being

axed. So he thought of a better—if a tad more radical—solution: He borrowed a National Guard chopper from a buddy and flew it over to Johnny's place. "I was asleep," recalls Johnny, "and [wife] **June** came in and woke me up, says, 'Some fool has landed a helicopter in your yard!' Went out, and it was Kris. He fell out of the helicopter with a tape in one hand and a beer in the other. I said, 'Anybody that would go this far, I'm gonna listen to your song.'" Sure as shootin', "Sunday Morning Coming Down" was a number-one hit for Cash (in 1970), and Kristofferson's star was born.

But going to extremes can get you into trouble, as **Loretta Lynn**'s daughters, **Patsy** and **Peggy** (better known as **The Lynns**) found out the hard way. In a fit of misguided ambition, they decided to give their first single a boost by calling radio stations, posing as their own fans and repeatedly requesting the record. It didn't take long for DJs to catch on, and they had to phone the Lynns' record company to get the girls to

Re-Hearse-al

David Allan Coe used to park his surefire attention-getter—a hearse with his name painted on its side—in front of the Ryman Auditorium on Opry night every week.

stop. And the **Dixie Chicks** were ousted from David Letterman's office building in New York after they crashed the place and gave the startled tenants an impromptu demonstration of their quite considerable talents—by breaking into song upon arrival!

Hard Hat Days and Honky-Tonk Nights

> "A lot of people never play their music outside of Nashville and come here green. It is not a very forgiving town. Make your mistakes somewhere else— somewhere that's kinder."
> (Tracy Lawrence)

Payin' your dues in the clubs is usually a required rung on the ladder to stardom. **BR5-49** got their big break playing a few shows a night in the picture window of a downtown Nashville boot store that also sidelined as a nightclub. The popular group soon came to the attention of record-company executives and nabbed a deal. What if you're not in Nashville? Native Texan **David Kersh** remembers some of his early experiences playing the local circuit: "You've heard of 'the sticks.' Well, some of these halls (I played) are in 'the twigs.'" **Trace Adkins** performed in the same kinds of dives. "The music I did in the clubs I called 'combat country,'" he recalls. "You've got to go in those clubs—especially in Texas, where I spent so much time—and play for fairly jaded audiences. You're not going to blow them away unless you do something different." Now, *different* doesn't necessarily mean *original*: "I wouldn't give up on (my music)," avers **Hal Ketchum**. "Not even when a club owner turned on the jukebox in the middle of one of my songs, or when somebody came up to me and said, 'You better play a **George Strait** song in the near future, *or else.*'"

It never hurts to have a pal or two in higher places. **Roger Miller** was mentored by bluegrass legend **Bill Monroe**, who "used to call me into his dressing room at the Opry and tell his band, 'Hey boys, listen to this kid.' I'd play my songs and he'd say, 'Ain't that great?'" When he first arrived in Nashville, **Jason Sellers** got a push from nice-guy **Vince Gill**: "I got this phone number from somebody. I called up expecting to hear, 'So and So Management' or whatever. And the voice said, 'Hey, this is Vince.' And I went, 'Vince. Somebody who is working at the desk that is answering the phone for Vince Gill. What a coincidence that y'all got the same name.' I had no idea it was his home phone number. But anyway, I just gave him my sales pitch. He encouraged me, gave me some work singing and playing bass, and later recommended me for a job playing with **Billy Joe Royal**. He was a big part of my career here getting cranked up, and I'll always be grateful to him for that." Whatta guy! And **Denise Jackson**, **Alan**'s wife, corraled **Glen Campbell** at an airport (she was working as a flight attendant), talked to him evah so sweetly, and finagled her soon-to-be-famous hubby a songwriting deal with the rhinestone cowboy's publishing concern.

"I told him, 'Son, I'd like to see you get out and ride [a horse] just a little bit, to where you'd feel more comfortable.'"
(**Garth Brooks**'s mom, who was worried her son might not be "country" enough)

Chris LeDoux, a gen-u-wine cowboy singer who'd been playing rodeos and clubs throughout the wide West for years, got a big boost when his name was mentioned in the lyric to **Garth Brooks**'s first single, "Much Too Young (To Feel This Damn Old)." After the record hit, LeDoux and Brooks got together and did a duet ("Whatcha Gonna Do With a Cowboy?"), which came about because ever-ambitious, image-conscious Brooks, according to LeDoux, "called me up and we started talkin' about how everyone wants to do a duet with him. But he said he wanted to do this song with me because he's not a real cowboy and he thought I'd give the thing more credibility." Wouldn't take much.

"I wanted to say, 'Done.' I tried everything. . . . I told my mom, 'I quit.' She let me go through my whole speech and said, 'Right. What are you going to do?' I thought about it and said, 'I'd better get back to work.'"
(**Marty Stuart**)

Take This Job and Shove It

"I nearly starved to death before I got a
job [in Nashville]. I'd tell people I came to
town to become a singer, and they
wouldn't hire me. I finally started lying
and said I was tone-deaf and not
interested in music—and
finally got some work."
(Faith Hill)

Born tired and raised lazy? Nope—here's how they made
ends meet before they were stars.

Roy Acuff: pro baseball player (had several unfortu-
nate sunstroke attacks, which laid him low for
months and ix-nayed his sports career)

Trace Adkins: pipe-fitter, oil worker, construction worker

Gary Allan: owned a construction company and worked
on a car lot

Bill Anderson: DJ, reporter

John Anderson: at age seventeen, worked as a carpenter
roofing the new Opryland

Eddy Arnold: mortuary assistant, ambulance driver

Stephanie Bentley: waitress, beauty-pageant contestant, jingle singer
(for Hardees restaurants, Southern Bell, and the Yellow Pages)

Clint Black: iron worker, fishing guide, bait cutter

James Bonamy: worked in rubber reclamation (**"It was the smelliest,
stinkiest stuff."** Sorta like his music.)

Garth Brooks: boot salesman, pizza maker, roofer

T. Graham Brown: jingle singer (for McDonald's, Taco Bell, Miller, and Budweiser)

Tracy Byrd: housepainter

Glen Campbell: garbage-truck driver

Deana Carter: waitress, nursery school teacher, janitor

Johnny Cash: appliance salesman

Kenny Chesney: valet, telemarketer, fire-hydrant tester

Mark Chesnutt: "I've always made a good living at [music], and other than a little time I spent bouncing back and forth between working at the lawn and garden center at Montgomery Ward and a job with a delivery company, it's all I've ever done."

Patsy Cline: drugstore clerk

John Conlee: funeral director, DJ

Rodney Crowell: dishwasher

Billy Ray Cyrus: car salesman, Chippendales dancer (denies)

Lacy J. Dalton: topless dancer (for two weeks)

Mac Davis: probation officer (during the same period, he says, he played in a band featured at "high school sock hops and fraternity puke-outs")

Joe Diffie: "I wanted to be a doctor. It sounds so weird, though—'Dr. Diffie to the operating room!'"

Donna Fargo: English teacher

Freddy Fender: mechanic

Jeff Foxworthy: computer engineer

Cleve Francis: cardiologist

Teddy Gentry (Alabama): carpet layer

Lee Greenwood: Las Vegas lounge singer and blackjack dealer

Merle Haggard: dishwasher, doughnut maker

Wade Hayes: construction worker

Ty Herndon: fast-food chef, jingle singer (for Dodge, Pepsi, and TNN)

Faith Hill: sold T-shirts at Fan Fair and answered phones for both **Gary Morris** and **Reba McEntire**

Alan Jackson: TNN mailroom clerk, staff writer for **Glen Campbell**'s music publishing company, construction worker, shoe salesman, furniture salesman (says being a singer is **"more exciting than driving a forklift, which is what I did a few years ago"**— for Kmart)

Waylon Jennings: DJ

George Jones: housepainter

Naomi Judd: nurse, secretary, model

Toby Keith: semipro football player, rodeo hand, oil worker

David Kersh: carpet store manager, wood floor installer, concrete layer, sewer worker

Sammy Kershaw: Wal-Mart remodeler, rice-factory worker, DJ

The Kinleys (Heather and Jennifer): waitresses, bartenders

Kris Kristofferson: military pilot, janitor

Tracy Lawrence: construction worker, telemarketer, grocery boy (**"As a teenager, I had a job packing grocery bags in Piggly Wiggly, and I'd be thinking, 'Where is George Strait tonight?'"**)

Mila Mason boasts, **"I was an extra in more than forty music videos. I was in R&B, rock, and country videos. I did a lot of those karaoke videos that were sent overseas. To add to my video income, I did modeling and TV commercials, including a national spot for Toyota."** Stellar, baby.

Kathy Mattea: tour guide at the Country Music Hall of Fame

Martina McBride: sold T-shirts at Garth Brooks concerts, then was hired as his opening act

Roger Miller: bellboy, bull rider, fireman (fired after sleeping through the second fire alarm of his short-lived career)

Willie Nelson: Bible salesman, vacuum cleaner salesman, plumber's assistant, plus, **"I considered preaching, but preachers don't make a lot, and they have to work hard."**

K. T. Oslin: Broadway chorus girl

Randy Owen (Alabama): carpet installer

Lee Roy Parnell: rancher, sales rep

Minnie Pearl: drama teacher

Charley Pride: baseball player, construction worker

Collin Raye: Las Vegas lounge singer

Ricky Van Shelton: pipe fitter

Hank Snow: cabin boy

Doug Stone: mechanic

George Strait: ranch hand (hey, wait a minute—he still is . . . of course, now it's on his own spread)

Mel Street: construction worker

Aaron Tippin: farm worker, welder, corporate pilot, truck driver, mechanic

Randy Travis: singer, dishwasher, construction worker, and cook at at the lovely **Lib Hatcher**'s Nashville Palace

Travis Tritt: heating and air-conditioning worker, truck driver, school-bus driver, mechanic (**"I worked construction, house-framing, made furniture, and worked at a printing company. I even got married twice and divorced twice by the time I turned twenty-two."**)

Clay Walker: ranch hand, janitor

Bryan White: T-shirt salesman

Hank Williams: peanut salesman, shoeshine boy

Bob Wills: hobo, barber, carpenter, car salesman, preacher

Tammy Wynette: beautician

Trisha Yearwood: receptionist (for MTM Records), demo singer

Dwight Yoakam: furniture mover, truck driver (he really doesn't *look* that macho)

A Boy Named Sue

ROYAL WADE

Kimes ("I tell you, I did talk to [my dad] a little bit about it when I got older. He had actually thought about my name for a long time and wanted to name me Wade but didn't have a first name picked out. Then he got desperate when I got here. I'd been home from the hospital for two days and he was in this café in Mulberry [Arkansas], where I was born, drinking coffee, and he looked up and saw this Royal Crown sign. He thought Royal would make a good first name and so that's who I became. I'm just glad he didn't see a Nehi sign!")

ALTON & RABON

(better known as the Delmore Brothers)

Swayde

(Neal McCoy's son)

CHELY

Wright (pronounced "Shelly")

STONEY

Edwards (born Frenchy Edwards)

GOLDIE

Hill (born Argolda Vancile Hill . . . no wonder she changed it)

TRACE

Adkins (named his daughter Mackenzie which, he says, means "daughter of the wise leader")

SHERRIÉ

Austin (pronounced Sher-EE . . . how continental)

MATRACA

Berg (pronounced "Muh-TRAY-suh", not "Muh-TRAH-cuh")

BOUDLEAUX

Bryant, songwriter ("Rocky Top")

PLANET & SIERRA

(Billy Swan's daughters)

Lari

White (pronounced "Laurie," God knows why)

TROYAL

(Garth's given name. Niiiiiice.)

RADNEY

Foster (a good ol' Southern boy-type moniker)

JO DEE

Messina (this name has to be two words?)

Icee

Berg (Matraca's mom, who used to play with her strangely named aunts—Sudie, Clara, and Coleida—as the Callaways)

Steelen

(Toby Keith's daughter)

KIPPI

Brannon (a good name for a small dog)

DEANA

Carter (pronounced "DEE-nuh," named after Dean Martin, for whom her father used to play guitar)

RHETT

Akins (named after Margaret Mitchell's Mr. Butler)

Fast Fact

Dolly, the cloned sheep, was named after the pneumatic Ms. Parton because the cells used in the process were taken from mammary glands.

One More Name

A Few of Country's More Colorful Monikers

The Best Friend a Song Ever Had: **Conway Twitty**

The Coal Miner's Daughter: **Loretta Lynn**

The Country Gentleman: **Chet Atkins**

The Country Sunshine Girl: **Dottie West**

The Possum; The Rolls Royce of Country Music: **George Jones**

The Drifting Cowboy; The Drifting Kid: **Hank Williams**

The Singing Brakeman: **Jimmie Rodgers**

The Singing Bronc Rider: **Chris LeDoux**

The Farmboy Charmboy: **Glen Campbell**

The First Lady of Country Music: **Tammy Wynette**

The Singing Fisherman: **Johnny Horton**

The Singing Ranger: **Hank Snow**

The Singing Sheriff: **Faron Young**

The High Priest of Country Music: **Conway Twitty**

The Hillbilly Shakespeare: **Hank Williams**

The Hip Hick: **Glen Campbell**

The Poet Laureate of the Working Man: **Merle Haggard**

The Thinking Man's Country Singer: **Earl Thomas Conley** (who admits, "Since I haven't recorded in seven years, I think I'm taking a little too long to think about it.")

2
Rags to Rhinestones

Mindy McCready: The new "class" in country

Rhinestone Cowboy

"Country has gone cute now: **Clint Black** is cute, **Billy Ray Cyrus** is cute, **Lyle Lovett** has since become cute. The quality of the music has gone down, but the cute factor has gone up."
(**Phil Kaufman**, veteran road manager)

To be a success back in the good ol' days, all you needed was a strong voice, a load of hard-won life experience, and a few heartfelt, heart-string-tuggin' ditties. That reality is a thing of the past, along with the prevailing wisdom that said it really didn't matter what you looked like as long as you could sing your little heart out. Gone also, for the most part anyway, are those colorfully tacky stage costumes—Scarlett O'Hara dresses, diamond-encrusted pinky rings, gaudy Nudie suits—that made country stars look like rustic bumpkins who'd fallen ass over teakettle into a vat of sequins.

"**I'd much rather they analyze my songs than my britches.**"
(**Kris Kristofferson**)

These days, you can't wear that stuff because, frankly, it leaves way too much to the imagination (although you're still expected to wear the olde-tymey duds if you're someone like **Loretta Lynn** or **Porter Wagoner**—in which case coverage is a definite plus). Sex sells—and the audience is buying, in droves. If you're a woman, you bare your booty and display maximum Grand Canyon frontage; if you're a man, you swath yourself in bluer-than-blue jeans that cling to your narrow butt like Saran Wrap, and you remember to take off your wedding ring for photo shoots. Hillbilly fashion plate **Marty Stuart** swears he'd "much prefer loose overalls and no underwear. But somewhere along the line some hillbilly discovered this sells records."

 "Billy Ray [Cyrus], he's not a good singer—but you don't need to be if you look that good."
(Waylon Jennings)

"So much of this business is about image," laments husky semihunk **Joe Diffie**. "You have to compete with the **Clint Black**s and **Alan Jackson**s. So you can't just sing—you have to look good, too." Bitter **Buck Owens** has noticed the same disheartening direction in today's music biz: "It seems like the first thing they say is, 'Well, how tall is he?' 'He's five-foot-eleven.' 'That's pretty good. How much does he weigh?' 'Well, he weighs 145.' 'That's good; he's slim, then. How's he look in jeans?' 'Well, he looks okay in jeans.' 'Does he wear a hat?' 'Yeah, he'll wear a hat if we want him to.' And the last thing they ask, 'Oh, by the way, can he sing?'"

 "Just 'cause I wear a hat ain't got a thing to do with where my head's at."
(Billy Joe Shaver)

The old **Garthster** (who, wrote one discerning scribe, has a face that looks like "a thumb with a hat on it") thinks he might be bucking this trend. "Three years ago," he asks, "would you have thought that the largest-selling artist in the '90s would be going bald and have an eating problem and be doing fiddle and steel guitar music?"

 "I don't think you're giving country fans much credit when you think they're gullible enough to buy something just because they like someone's looks."
(John Michael Montgomery)

Hey! Somebody stole the bottom half of Alan's jacket!

Überhunk **Alan Jackson**'s wife, Denise, says, "I never dreamed my husband would be the heartthrob of America, but it makes me feel good that I spotted him all those years ago." Alan doesn't quite concur with her assessment: "Nobody screamed for me when I was drivin' that forklift except the boss." And his pin-up public image doesn't sit quite right with him either: "When I see myself on video I think I look more goofy than anything. Anyone who's long and tall feels real awkward, because you can't walk cool like some guy who's 5'11" . . . you just move weird, which is why I always felt more like Gomer on *The Andy Griffith Show* than a sex symbol." (Yeah right—try telling that to your zillions of hopelessly devoted female fans.) **Vince Gill**, who has wrestled with a weight problem throughout much of his career, feels the same way: "I don't think my fan base looks at me as a heartthrob like some of these other guys. I've got a little bit of Gomer in me." (Sorry, Vince, but **Pam Tillis** had it right when she called you "perfection on two legs.") On the other hand, stick figure **Ronnie Dunn**, according to pudgy partner **Kix Brooks**, is not real concerned about his image—in fact, he has one of Music Row's lighter workout regimens: "He turns his treadmill on and watches it run."

"There's a lot of good-looking women in country music right now, and I like that."
(Johnny Cash)

On the distaff side, the country universe is populated by a big bunch of bodacious babes: **Faith**, **Shania**, **Mila**, **Mindy**, and their comely kin. Former bombshell **K. T. Oslin** observes, "I sometimes feel like we've come a long, long way and that the doors are opening, and then the next day I think the only thing we have achieved is the right to take off more clothes in order to get the gig." Queen of Tackiness **Lorrie Morgan** protests that, "I don't consider myself a sexpot or anything like that . . . but I don't think there's anything wrong in dressing and

"I refuse to play down the way I look in order to be taken seriously as an artist."
(Shania Twain)

looking like a woman." I see—apparently "looking like a woman" means showing as much skin as you can without getting arrested, in the flimsiest of feather-n-fur-furled get-ups, together with flaunting your multiple body-piercings—both Morgan and her young daughter have fetchingly pierced navels (as does **Mindy McCready**), and Lorrie also pierced her nose. How . . . feminine.

> **"They wanted me to be glamorous; I wanted to be more natural. I get manipulation that would not happen with a male artist. The trend has always been that women need help from a man. I get that more because I'm only twenty-two years old."**
> **(Mindy McCready)**

It would be hard to find anyone in country that bares more than shapely **Shania Twain**, who, when she was a star on the rise, hired Hollywood cheesecake experts **John** and **Bo Derek** to help craft her ooh-la-la image (according to Ms. Twain, "[John] sees me and I'm like a monster to him. It wasn't funny at the time. 'Somebody give me a knife!' he said. 'I've got to cut that nose off!'"). However, she warns, "don't let this frilly look fool you." Okay, let's all just focus on her *wonderful songs*, shall we? "I am the last person you'll see in a string bikini on the beach. I'm not a *Baywatch* girl," she adds. "The bottom line is that people are digging the music, and that's the most gratifying." Twain also confesses she "used to be very insecure about having large breasts." So glad she got over *that*.

> **"The most I've ever shown is my midriff, and I'm quite comfortable with my midriff. It's like a man showing off his arms or something."**
> **(Shania Twain)**

Older and Bolder

"Wouldn't it be great to be a woman and be just like **Willie Nelson**? I've often thought, God, would that be great—to be the first woman out there with wrinkles and not trying to cover it up."
(K. T. Oslin)

Now, what happens when bonny belles begin the inevitable slide into middle age? Well, some think they've still got it—**Dottie West**, for one. She posed for the fine "gentlemen's" magazine *Oui* at age fifty! Not all timeworn temptresses have such an unflagging sense of self-confidence, however. **Tammy Wynette** felt that the care and feeding of one's image was "very important for anybody in the limelight, whether it be a hair transplant, a boob job, a face-lift, nose changed, eyes—whatever. I would do it." **Reba McEntire**, after consulting with good pal and plastic-surgery poster

child **Dolly Parton** (who admits "Yes, I've had several little things done . . . and several big ones!"), recently went under the knife for a little touch-up. "I don't see any reason to sag into the cement," she explains about her eye job. And **K. T. Oslin** had a face-lift to "allow me to have some control over the way I looked on camera." Well, all right—used sparingly, plastic surgery can erase a few years of hard living from almost any craggy mug. But oh-so-taut, puffy-lipped **Tanya Tucker**(ed) appears to have gone waaaay too far—though she's never publicly admitted to having had anything done, her features now bear only a passing resemblance to her former face (see pages 42–43). She should have taken Dolly's advice—though Miss Parton is never "delighted to be talking about this," she warns that one should do some research on plastic surgeons beforehand so one doesn't come out looking "like a banjo head." Oops! Too late!

The "old" Tanya

The "new" (older) Tanya

Dolly's Beauty Secrets

"PMS ain't nothing compared to going on a diet."

"What do I weigh? I just always say a hundred and plenty."

"I wasn't born with a wig and makeup, and I could be very stylish if I chose to be. But I would never stoop so low as to be <u>fashionable</u>."

"I'm not offended by all the dumb-blonde jokes because I know that I'm not dumb. I also know that I'm not blond."

"I look like the girl next door—if you happen to live next door to an amusement park."

"Yeah, I see [old shows with Porter Wagoner] once in a while, and I just fall over. I can't hardly stand to watch myself like that. I think, 'Oh, my God, look at that hair!' Then I look in the mirror at it now and I think, 'Oh lord, it's still there!'"

How tall is Dolly? Five feet even, or "6'4", with wigs and heels."

"It's a good thing that I was born a woman, or I'd have been a drag queen."

"I patterned my look after Cinderella, Mother Goose, and the local hooker."

"Lots of women buy just as many wigs and makeup and things as I do . . . they just don't wear them all at the same time."

"I look artificial,
but I'm not."
(Dolly Parton)

She Don't Know She's Beautiful

A little self-reflection is good for the soul, especially when one is pondering such weighty topics as one's superficial appearance.

**"My boobs are too saggy, and the kids call me 'Weenie Butt.'"
(Tammy Wynette)**

**"I've got a beer belly, no muscles, and I'm bowlegged as hell."
(John Michael Montgomery)**

**"I don't see anything particular in the mirror. Pretty plain. Pretty simple. I have good teeth. . . . My eyes are too small. Have good cheekbones. My legs are stumpy. Dented nose."
(Shania Twain)**

**"I hate and loathe my hands. My fingers are short and fat—yuck!"
(Sara Evans)**

**"I've always had a pretty darn perky figure."
(Loretta Lynn)**

**"I'm an American female—I mean, the Barbie syndrome. It's like, I will never live up to that. I'm so hypercritical of myself. I always have to lose the proverbial five pounds. Isn't that sad? It's not like I'm a teenager and should have a twenty-two-inch waist anymore."
(Deana Carter)**

Looks Aren't Everything

When asked about their worst features, the stars spoke out candidly. Sammy Kershaw hates his "short legs," Billy Dean despises his "puffy eyes," Lila McCann can't stand "My top lip—it disappears when I smile," and Ruby Lovett laments her "big ol' gut," as does Mark Wills, who can't abide his "beer gut—and I don't even drink!"

Country-Wide

> *"I like the feel of a little weight. I gives me a sense of being centered and steady."*
> **(K. T. Oslin)**

Despite the grumbling we've heard about looks being too all-fired important, hill-billy celebs are the first ones at the gym every morning. They don't really have any choice—if they don't keep up appearances, they'll soon be replaced by the next Kountry Ken or Hillbilly Barbie that Nashville's tastemakers decide to foist on us.

When one is inclined toward a little extra poundage, as many country folks are, one must take steps to control it. **Garth Brooks**, who was up to about 240 pounds at one point, just cut out junk food to lose weight; whale-size **Wynonna** lost twenty-five pounds on Slim-Fast (and was being considered for a spokesmodel position—possibly nixed by the fact that she can't seem to *keep* it off). When he first got into the music biz, 5'10" **Joe Diffie** weighed about 260 pounds, which almost KO'd his career before it began. "One executive told me that if I looked like **George Strait**, he'd sign me immediately," Diffie recalls, "but that I needed to lose weight." Which he did—he must be down to about 252 now.

Phone-sex purveyor **Kenny Rogers** took a more direct route to losing the tonnage he'd packed on through the years. About his liposuction procedure, which took off twenty-five pounds and eleven inches from Rogers's gargantuan girth, he says, "It was probably a middle-age crisis. You suddenly see those first gray hairs. Then you get reviews that begin by talking about your weight. When I first brought up the possibility of liposuction, my (now former) wife Marianne said, 'I can't believe you. I never thought you noticed such things.' Well, I didn't when I was twenty-five, but things change."

An ultraflattering profile shot of the suddenly svelte
Mr. Rogers

Buttons and Bows

 "In country music's history, when it comes to fashion, there's a few years we'd rather forget."
(Marty Stuart)

The country club has never exactly been famed for its subtlety, either musically or sartorially. In fact, it's usually been just the opposite: The more red-white-and-blue-sequined stripes, big ol' gold nuggets, frills, flounces, flares, star-spangled petticoats, and ruffles an outfit has, the better.

 "I've never had anybody tell me something was too much." (Country tailor-to-the-stars **Manuel**, creator of gaudy get-ups like Porter Wagoner's sequined-wheel-bedecked jackets— which, by the way, Porter charges fans a buck to be photographed in!)

So is this preference for over-the-top costumery changing? Well, maybe, maybe not. For **Mama Judd**'s farewell concert, deciding what to wear, she says, didn't take much ruminatin'. "I knew only my red vinyl party dress with crinolines would do. . . . If Scarlett O'Hara took the green curtains off the window and wore them, then this is like I took the red vinyl seat covers off my '57 Chevy."

 "I've worked so hard to keep this from being a gender thing that I've had to learn to be more comfortable with the part of me that is female and sexual. And I've finally learned to stop buttoning my blouses up to the chin."
(Kathy Mattea)

Loretta Lynn in her ruffle-drenched Sunday best

Die-hard fashion victim **Reba McEntire** took the advice of her more sophisticated handlers and dumped her "tiddleywink tops—the ones with big chunks of sequins on them" in favor of a sleeker, more classy look, along with a pixie haircut that makes her look like she's three years old.

> **"I had wanted to cut it [her large, puffy red mop] for three years, but kept hearing, 'No, the fans won't like it.' It got too old looking for me. I wanted to be the little frisky person that I was and have my hair reflect that. So I went in and looked at a lot of pictures, and I chose one of Meg Ryan on the cover of some big magazine."**
> **(Reba McEntire)**

Now, some of this type of olde-tymey, feather-boa fluffery and rhinestone cowgirl tomfoolery is just for fun. The **Dixie Chicks**, for example, used to wear nothin' but Western duds. But, says **Martie Seidel**, "when people started coming to our shows more concerned about what outfit we were going to wear instead of what song we were going to play, we said, 'Whoa.'" And when **Lorrie Morgan** went on tour with **Pam Tillis** and **Carlene Carter** (none of whom are known for their taste . . . or at least their *good* taste), she said they had a ball checking out each other's closets: "It's always fun to watch everybody come out," she said, "because you're like, 'What do you have on? What shoes? Oh, I hate you!'"

> **"Country went shopping."**
> **(Clint Black**, on the new "class" in country wardrobes)

How to Look Like Bryan White

(. . . not that you'd want to)

Ultrawimp **Bryan White** uses a scrub and moisturizer on his pink-cheeked face; when his little round eyes get puffy, he applies cucumber slices. "It really works," he squeaks.

High As the Mountains

"I came so close at the beginning of
the year to getting a mohawk."
(Billy Ray Cyrus)

The crowning glory of any country star
is his or her hair. Whether it's long or short
(it's *never* in-between), more time and care
is spent in pursuit of tonsorial transcendence than on
boot-polishin', buckle-buffin', makeup application (although it runs a close second), or anything else.
Now, this isn't necessarily a bad thing, but
the effort involved in the care and feeding of
one's locks can be taken to ridiculous extremes. **Crystal Gayle**'s Rapunzel-like 'do is,
she admits, "a chore. Taking care of it is a
nightmare."

"I have to keep washing
and blow-drying it. If it
gets too high, I start to look
like an evangelist."
(Bryan White)

One way to get around the hassle is to wear wigs. **Loretta Lynn**
reportedly started puttin' 'em on when overzealous fans started snip-
ping off hunks of her hair to take home for souvenirs (blech). **Dolly
Parton** has her own line of the thangs, which are so fabulous that their
namesake guarantees, "If you don't look great, I'll refund your pur-
chase price!" (Can she get her own money back?)

"I'm proud it's completely gray, and I'm not
going to bother with coloring it because I
have other things to do with my time."
(Emmylou Harris)

The Long and Short of It

What's the deal with **Lyle Lovett's 'do?**

"Well, I guess the haircut is a trademark, but it was unintentional. The reason for it originally was I went on this tour with Bonnie Raitt for about two months and I didn't get a haircut, and all of a sudden people were writing about my hair. And I thought, 'This is a pretty easy way to [get attention].' So I sort of left it."

"I think my hair is only unusual in the context of country music."

"I really don't believe that I'm the only person in country music with this kind of hair. All those guys who wear hats—**Dwight Yoakam, George Strait**—actually have hair just like mine."

When **Julia Roberts** wed Lyle, the crew members on her movie set had T-shirts made that said, "He's a lovely boy . . . but you really must do something about that hair!"

The Hairbilly Hall of Shame

The Curl Up and Dye Pile-up
(a.k.a. Big Hair)
Worn by: Dolly Parton, Reba McEntire, Loretta Lynn, Tammy Wynette
Usually seen on: redneck hillbilly queens dripping with jewelry; fortyish beauty salon employees

Sexy Ragamuffin
Worn by: Shania, Mindy, Lorrie
Usually seen on: anyone who just rolled out of bed

Neo-Retro Punk Mop
Worn by: Rosanne Cash, Marty Stuart
Usually seen on: folks who were really hip about twenty years ago

"When I was playin' in them dives, it got to where I just never did get my hair cut."
(Alan Jackson)

Redneck Cover-up
(a.k.a. I'm a little bit country; I'm a little bit rock 'n' roll)
Worn by: Tracy Lawrence, Travis Tritt, Alan Jackson
Usually seen on: rural auto mechanics, peeking out from underneath a greasy Caterpillar Tractor baseball cap

The Brave-Little-Sioux Pigtail
Worn by: Billy Ray Cyrus, Willie Nelson
Usuallys seen on: squaws

The Sprayed-into-Submission, Unmoving Swirls
Worn by: Glen Campbell, Kenny Rogers, George Jones, Little Jimmy Dickens
Usually seen on: televangelists

Eyes Big As Dallas

Country's Must-Have Grooming Skills

Belly-button-ring-buffing
Bikini-waxing
Eyeliner-painting
Eyeshadow-shoveling
Belt-cinching
Bang-curling
Fall-/weave-placing

Nail-glue application
Jewelry-fastening
Eyelash-curling
Pancake-troweling
Beehive adornment

Teasing
Backcombing
Hairspraying
Blowdrying
Bobby-pinning
Wig-fluffing
False-eyelash-gluing

3

Gone Country

The Country Club

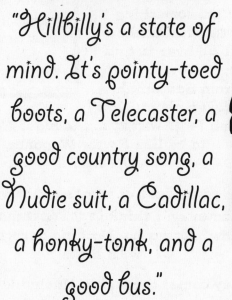

"Hillbilly's a state of mind. It's pointy-toed boots, a Telecaster, a good country song, a Nudie suit, a Cadillac, a honky-tonk, and a good bus."

(Marty Stuart)

What's Country?

"What do you mean [it's] peasant music, you goddamned son of a bitch!"
(Faron Young, to Zsa Zsa Gabor)

"Country is soul music for white people."
(Paul Shaffer)

"Country music is shit. It just isn't honest anymore. A cat gets out there onstage with a fancy suit on, something made by Nudie with feathers and sequins all over it, and he's wearing a cowboy hat and he's from Savannah, Georgia, man. It's phony. How can you sell Porter Wagoner to the kids? Nobody wants to be like Porter Wagoner."
(Joe South)

"You have your ideas of what's country: I think Hank Williams is country; I think Garth Brooks may not be, you know? Ha ha ha. Nothing derogatory."
(Willie Nelson)

"If the money comes through a Nashville bank, then it's country."

(John D. Loudermilk)

What's Yore Style? ♪ **Bluegrass**

(a.k.a. "the High Lonesome Sound")

Honky. Twangy. Stringy. Named after Kentucky-native/bluegrass legend Bill Monroe's band, the Blue Grass Boys.

"Bluegrass music is basically a back-porch music. It's music that you play to entertain yourself, your fiddle and your banjo."
(Marty Stuart)

What's Yore Style? ♪ **Contemporary Country**

Pop by any other name. Just about everything that's played on country radio these days: Shania, LeAnn, Faith, Garth, Trisha, Tim McGraw.

"Country music speaks emotional truth. Rock has drifted from it."
(Camille Paglia)

Categorically Speaking

"I don't know if you could call my music cowboy music. I don't sing about horses."
(Merle Haggard)

"Someone told me once that our music was like a large-mouth bass at a catfish dinner."
(Mark Orr, Kentucky Headhunters)

"It's hard for me to know what category to put it all in. I had a song called 'Down on My Knees,' and someone [on the radio] made the comment that it was not country enough. Then fine, play George Jones—which they don't. They say I'm not country enough, but then they won't play the traditional country-music singers that are still making records."
(Trisha Yearwood)

"Country listeners are getting younger and younger. They don't know this is a jacked-up '90s version of Connie Smith and Loretta Lynn."
(Chely Wright)

"It's heartbreaking for me because I love [traditional country], and it's just hard to accept hearing somebody say [my music] is too country for country radio."
(Lee Ann Womack)

What's Yore Style? ♫ Outlaw

"I think the outlaw movement came with people who got tired of bein' told how to do things. Back then, there was a certain way you were supposed to dress. There was a certain kind of song you were supposed to sing. The movement came when we said, 'We don't care what you say; that's the way we're gonna do it.' Because we did that, we became what was known as 'outlaws.' "
(Johnny Paycheck)

What's Yore Style? ♫ Western

(a.k.a. Singing Cowboys)
Not just country singers dressing up like cowboys, but music, performed by folks like Roy Rogers and the Sons of the Pioneers, with Western themes (the life of a 'poke, riding the range, long trail drives, pans o' beans, ladies o' the evenin'). Aficionados of the genre really resent it if you call their music country, so don't.

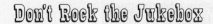

Don't Rock the Jukebox

"Most people don't realize it, but when we were getting started we were these guys in T-shirts with long hair and their guitars, all jumping around on stage, and we were really frowned on."
(Randy Owen, Alabama)

"Back when I first started, in the late '50s, I rocked out a little. Somebody—I won't say who it was—came to me and told me, 'Hoss . . . you got to understand the difference between country music and that rock 'n' roll. In country music we want wet eyes, not wet crotches.' "
(Bobby Bare)

"There's a lot of people out there that hated country music before, that are really diggin' it because of [rock 'n' roll]. And so I think it's good to have a traditional side and a rock 'n' roll and pop side of country music."
(Bryan White)

"Rock 'n' roll's killing us all."
(Faron Young)

"I never wanted to be restricted by any genre's standards. That's one of the beauties of pop. Pop is everything. In America especially, country music is still very, very exclusive."
(Shania Twain)

"I don't want to be a pop singer."
(Tracy Lawrence)

"I never ever left country music. I just took it with me."
(Dolly Parton)

What's Yore Style? ♪ **Honky-Tonk**

Hard-edged country themes, like adultery, divorce, and *partyin' down, man,* for dissolute grown-ups. Also, any whiskey joint where dissolute grown-ups go to listen to boot-scootin' country music.

What's Yore Style? ♪ *Urban Cowboy*

Popularized by that famous buckaroo from New Jersey, John Travolta, in the movie of the same name. Boots. Bolos. Big hats. Blue jeans. Oh yeah, and a few dumb songs about riding mechanical bulls.

"I don't know anything about crossover. We have always claimed to operate under the flag of country music."
(Garth Brooks)

"My music is already pop, I think, in the sense that it is popular."
(Shania Twain)

"Pop will play you for about four months, wear you out, and then throw you out like a piece of trash."
(Garth Brooks)

"I couldn't go pop with a mouthful of firecrackers."
(Waylon Jennings)

"They're leaving cheating songs out. They don't have songs about drinking anymore. And more people are drinking and cheating today than they was back then. What they've done is took the heart and soul out of country music."
(George Jones)

"Young people don't necessarily like to cry in their beer these days as much as they like to dance."
(Willie Nelson)

New Attitudes

"Country music is about real life. Not all of life is about drinking and leaving your wife and having a dog and a truck."
(Mindy McCready)

"I don't gamble or go to bars. And I've got lots of time to, like, find a man or whatever."
(Lila McCann)

"I want to show people who don't dig country that it's not all songs about drinking and cheating on your wife."
(Bryan White)

This Business of Music

Repeat after me: "Country is a business." And, as with any other business, the most important thing is the bottom line—a fact that even the most individualistic performer must keep in mind.

"The audience that watches any kind of television and listens to any kind of audio gets the top quality just through ads. Hey, they have to be able to go from a Coke ad or a Janet Jackson record to my record and not notice the difference in quality. There's no reason we shouldn't be at that level. That's absolutely been my goal from the beginning."
(Shania Twain)

"You've got to be slick enough and clever enough to get through to the industry, and at the same time you've got to be simple and honest enough to get through to the public."
(Billy Dean)

Good luck with that one, BD.

"My goal has always been to be international."
(Shania Twain)

"I figure as an artist the best thing you can do is just follow your heart, and if your heart is marketable then you win."
(Rodney Crowell)

What's Yore Style? ♪ **Hard Country**

(a.k.a. Classic Country or Traditional Country)
Fiddles, pedal steel guitars, and traditional honk and twang. Think George Jones in a drinkin' mood, Garth's hero George Strait, and on the distaff side, Reba and Loretta.

What's Yore Style? ♪ **New Traditional**

Olde-tyme country style, gussied up some, both musically and lyrically (less about drinkin' and cheatin', more about loooooove) for contemporary ears...like **Randy Travis**.

"This is a business that's not very good about making people grow. It's kind of like high school with a lot of money."
(Radney Foster)

"What I am saying to all you songwriters is to get yourself a good Jewish lawyer before you sign anything, no matter how much the company says they love you."
(Willie Nelson)

"I don't intend to be bullied around by critics, by record companies, and by businessmen. Businessmen have nothing to do with my music. They can count all they want to, but they are not gonna put me in the numbers business. Let people get to where they don't want to listen. I'll entertain what's left."
(Tom T. Hall)

"You have to have four things to even have a chance in this music business. To start with, you need the dream, the desire to burn bright. You need the talent to back up that dream and the guts to be true to yourself about it. And you need persistence—persistence to stay and stay, to stick it through. But the fourth and most important thing is that you need to be blind, deaf, and dumb."
(Eddie Rabbitt)

Country State of Mind

> "I think country music has made it known
> that they're pretty much not interested in
> my music."
> (Emmylou Harris)

Country radio doesn't favor the old guard, and that sad fact has created a lot of resentment in veteran performers. **George Jones** calls it age discrimination. **Johnny Cash** agrees, and recently decided to let everyone know just how he felt. After winning a 1997 Grammy Award for his album *Chains*, he took out a full-page ad in music-biz trade rag *Billboard*. The piece featured a photo of Johnny along with this heartfelt message: "American Recordings and Johnny Cash would like to acknowledge the Nashville music establishment and country radio for your support." What was Johnny doing in the picture? Flipping the bird.

> "I don't think you could any more train a person
> to be a country singer than you could train
> someone to have almond eyes."
> (Merle Travis)

What about the non-Nashvilleans who have made country records? Some have done surprisingly well, including **Neil Diamond**, **Barbi** "Hef's honey" **Benton**, moaner-groaner **Bob Dylan**, and plain-vanilla TV hunk **John Schneider**. Others have humiliated themselves, like embarrassingly exhibitionistic actress **Sean** (*No Way Out*) **Young**, who attempted to jump-start her musical career with an ill-advised appearance at a concert in Ohio. According to Lisa Rebecca Gubernick, author of *Get Hot or Go Home*, a book on the making of **Trisha Yearwood**'s career, "[Sean]

Sting Has Stung

"Hey Sting, can we call you 'Stang'?"

(**Vince Gill**, after hearing Sting sing a duet with **Toby Keith** at the '97 CMA Awards)

did three songs, two up-tempo, one ballad. All were originals, none was on key.
She pranced around the stage, dancing
something that looked like a cross between
the two-step and the Swim. Mercifully, that has
been the last heard of Young's new career." (Next
on the list: **LaToya Jackson**, whose husband-
manager promises to transform her into "country's
next heartthrob"— yep, Music Row has always giv-
en a big hearty welcome to people who drape
themselves with snakes and have freak siblings
who wear surgical masks and sleep in oxygen
chambers.)

Successful outsiders are not given the full
benefit of that famous Southern hospitality—in fact,
they're usually met with outright resentment from the Nashville establishment, as happened when **Olivia Newton-John** won the Country Music
Association's Entertainer of the Year award in 1974, triggering comments like "She couldn't drawl with a mouth full of biscuits" **(Johnny
Paycheck)**. And when **John Denver**'s name appeared as the winnner of
the same award in 1975, presenter **Charlie Rich** torched the envelope
and its contents in protest (to read about the inventive excuse he used
to explain away the incident, see page 209).

Real Good Feel Good Song

Classic Country Song Themes

Trains 🎸 Trucks 🎸 Cars 🎸 Buses 🎸 Motorcycles 🎸 Motors 🎸 Workin' for a
livin' 🎸 Dead-end jobs 🎸 Drinkin' 🎸 Partyin' 🎸 Honky-tonkin' 🎸 Dancin' 🎸
Romancin' 🎸 Lovin' 🎸 Lost love 🎸 Found love 🎸 Good love 🎸 Bad love 🎸
Hubba-hubba love 🎸 Dead love 🎸 Cheatin' 🎸 Revenge 🎸 Divorce 🎸 Patriotism
🎸 Southern solidarity 🎸 Rednecks 🎸 Christmas 🎸 Famous dead people 🎸 Jesus
🎸 Mama 🎸 Heroes 🎸 Outlaws 🎸 Cowboys 🎸 Rodeos 🎸 Poverty 🎸 Jail time
🎸 Death in the family (younger sibling) 🎸 Death of any young 'un 🎸 Death in the
family (mama) 🎸 Death in the family (hard workin' daddy) 🎸 Death by broken
heart 🎸 Death by unnatural means (crashes and wrecks) 🎸 Heaven 🎸 Angels

If I Could Write a Song As Beautiful As You

"You got to have smelt a lot of mule manure before you can sing like a hillbilly."
(Hank Williams)

Where do country songwriters get their ideas? Well, real life is usually a pretty good place to start. **Deana Carter** wrote "Did I Shave My Legs for This?" in honor of a bottom-feeder boyfriend who was sponging off her ("I was with this person who didn't pay too much attention to me," Deana recalls. "Victoria's Secret, candles, and food did not faze this man."). **Dolly Parton** penned "I Will Always Love You" after splitting with puffy-pated **Porter Wagoner** both professionally and personally (the melancholic monster hit is, she says, "the song that bought me a lot of wigs"). And **Collin Raye**'s hit "I Can Still Feel You" was penned by his ex-girlfriend, Tammy Hyler—a fact he says he was ignorant of when he chose the song. "I heard the lyrics, and I thought, 'That sounds like what just happened to me,'" he says. "It took me a while to get used to the idea of singing it. At first, there's that embarrassed feeling, like if somebody took a bad picture of you and it showed up in print." **Billy Ray Cyrus** penned a hit tune, "Wher'm I Gonna Live," in response to an incident when his wife, tired of his staying out late and leaving her at home, chucked all of his belongings (probably a ton of hair products) onto their front lawn. **Bobbie Cryner** gets her inspiration in a slightly more down-home way: "I wrap my head in aluminum foil and sit on top of a mobile home." (You know you're a redneck country star if . . .)

"Women are the best things in the world to write about. They got it all—so what better subject than women? Oh, and whiskey?"
(songwriter **Dean Dillon**)

Toby Keith wrote "Should've Been a Cowboy" after a humiliating incident at a honky-tonk, where he gave the old come-on to a comely woman and she turned him down flat. Later the same night, he saw her cuttin' a rug with a dude decked out in buckaroo duds, prompting Toby to sigh, "I should've been a cowboy."

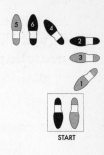

START   START

 "It can be explained in just one word: sincerity. When a hillbilly sings a crazy song, he feels crazy. When he sings, 'I laid my mother away,' he sees her a-laying right there in the coffin."
(Hank Williams)

Can you really sing about the country lifestyle if you haven't suffered . . . er, lived through it? **Emmylou Harris** wasn't so sure about that when she started out, so she wrote to one of her idols, folkie **Pete Seeger**, to ask if he thought she could have a career without doin' a lotta sufferin' (evidently his response was positive, 'cause she's still at it). **Willie Nelson** maintains that a long spell of tough times provided the idea for one of his depression-drenched ditties. "**Hank Cochran** and I had been sitting in the basement writing songs," he remembers. "That year I went through a divorce and had four cars wrecked. We were kicking all this around and we wrote a song: 'What Can You Do to Me Now?' The next day my house burned down." ("By the time I got there, it was burning real good," Willie remembers. "But I had this pound of Colombian grass inside. I wasn't being brave running in there to get my dope—I was trying to keep the firemen from finding it and turning me over to the police!")

 "Sometimes you don't realize how true country songs are until you find yourself in the middle of one."
(Hank Williams, Jr.)

"I don't like love songs that drizzle with sap and syrup.
The guys I've been around most of my life don't want to
be crawling on their knees, whinin', 'Please don't leave
me, honey.' A man's got his pride, you know?"
(Chris LeDoux)

"Let's face it—my songs are not syrupy. They haven't
got a lot of molasses poured on them."
(Buck Owens)

"It worked out because my fans were living the same
thing I was living—and they're still living it. They're still
having babies, ain't they? Men are still stepping out on
women. Women are still stepping out on men. There's still
a tavern open."
(Loretta Lynn)

"I used to like country," contends professional freak **Dennis Rodman** (a most discerning patron of the arts), "'til it really got me depressed when I listened to the words. If you listen to the words, you hear, 'Sorry I left you, honey, for screwing another girl,' or 'The truck killed the dog,' and those are depressing lyrics." D'oh! Heartbreak is a staple of the genre, dude. "Happy people don't write songs," explains **Harlan Howard**, one of country's all-time great tunesmiths. **Tim McGraw** concurs: "Everybody likes to write heartache songs whether they're having heartache or not."

"Country was too sad for me. My all-time favorite
artist isn't even country—it's **Lionel Richie**."
(Clay Walker)

"I still love to sing those [drinking] songs.
There's a lot of feeling in those types of songs.
It's almost like a cheating song."
(George Jones)

Got to Be Real

I Love You, George!

"If we could all sound like we wanted to, we'd all sound like George Jones."
(Waylon Jennings)

"You mean, besides George Jones?"
(Johnny Cash's stock answer when asked to name his favorite country performers)

"He's almost a godlike figure to me."
(Garth Brooks, who's almost a godlike figure to himself, too)

"George is the biggest hero I have in music."
(Sammy Kershaw)

"I love George Jones."
(bumper sticker on Alan Jackson's truck)

"I love Alan Jackson."
(bumper sticker on George Jones's identical truck)

"George Jones is the world's greatest country singer. George Jones reaches in and takes your heart out while it's pounding and shows it to you. And is kind enough to give it back."
(Hal Ketchum)

"I feel like I've just experienced a country song."
(Jason Sellers, after his car was broken into on his birthday)

"I put the hurtful things in my songs. It's better than a psychiatrist."
(Dolly Parton)

"I'd say that ninety-nine percent of what I write has come from my own experience. A person could probably start from my first song and go all the way to my last, and—if he knew what to look for—write my autobiography [sic]."
(Willie Nelson)

"Whether it's divorce or cancer in your family, I don't think you can sing from a mountaintop until you've been down in the bottom of the valley."
(T. G. Sheppard)

"Sometimes I joke that I'm gonna go out and get married and divorced so I can come up with the next album."
(Travis Tritt)

"I tend to average about ten hit songs per ex-wife."
(Vern Gosdin)

You just ain't lived enough, son

I Love You, Hag!

"He is one of the biggest reasons that I moved to Nashville and am a country singer today."
(John Anderson)

"Everybody wants to write a song like Merle Haggard."
(Alan Jackson)

"Back in my drinkin' days, whenever I wanted to get a beer and sit down and listen to some music, I always listened to Merle. I think Hag's one of the pillars of this industry."
(Johnny Paycheck)

"For me, as a songwriter, it was Merle Haggard. The emotion he put into his music was probably bad for him—but good for all of us out there listening."
(Kix Brooks)

"I was a Merle Haggard fanatic when I was growing up."
(Billy Dean)

"He had the whole package. He even had the name. Merle Haggard is a great country name. That's a country star."
(Toby Keith)

"I stay married until I run out of songs."
(songwriting great **Harlan Howard**, one of Music Row's most-hitched men)

"My father is a huge country-music fan. We sort of butted heads. He said, 'Be lookin' for songs,' and I said, 'I wanna write the songs.' He said, 'You haven't done enough livin'. You haven't spent enough time in barrooms to write real country songs.'"
(Clint Black)

"Dad would explain that it was a sad song, and I would sing it that way. I don't think I have to experience anything to sing it."
(LeAnn Rimes)

"If you're going to sing a sad song or a ballad, you've got to have lived it yourself."
(George Jones)

"If you had to live everything you sing, you'd be 150 years old before you could start recording."
(Barbara Mandrell)

"When people ask me if I live my records, I say, 'If I did, I'd be in prison or in a mental institution.'"
(Moe Bandy)

"I've lived my songs too strongly."
(George Jones)

T-R-O-U-B-L-E

Despite the focus on down-home values, country stars aren't immune to controversy. **Loretta Lynn**'s "The Pill" caused quite a stir when it was released in 1975, being just a little too far ahead of its time on the then-sensitive issue of birth control. **Garth Brooks**'s "The Thunder Rolls," which he made into a mini-movie music video about an abused wife who resolves her problems by killing her husband, was banned by both TNN and CMT because the stations' execs felt GB should take responsibility for its implied social statement. Said TNN: "The depiction of domestic violence is excessive and without an acceptable resolution." So they asked him to tape a short public service announcement ("You *can* get help; call this number" blah blah blah) to tack onto the end of the clip, which he did—but then inexplicably refused to let them air the durn thing. Artistic integrity? 'Fraid not. Prevailing wisdom was that the label's powers-that-be were convinced the brouhaha would be good for the tune (it doesn't seem to have hurt—it went straight to number one). Said Garth stiffly, "TNN has standards; I have standards. On this occasion, the two did not cross."

"All my songs are about sex. Nashville likes to pretend it doesn't exist. They should loosen up. Everyone's doing it, aren't they?"
(Mindy McCready)

Holly Dunn's "Maybe I Mean Yes" (which includes the immortal "When I say no I mean maybe/Or maybe I mean yes") was roundly denounced by the National Organization for Women (NOW), whose president huffed, "This kind of entertainment validates the ideas that women don't mean what they say." **Doug Supernaw** suffered similar slings and arrows of outrageous criticism when he vilified none other than the "biggest little city in the world," Reno, which objected to his song of the same name because it dares to compare a hard-hearted woman to a coldhearted gambling town. Gee, that's a stretch. Supernaw remembers that, "the mayor made comments and the city council said I didn't put their city in a very good light." Lighten up, folks! (Besides, anyone who's been there knows he's right.)

Cryin' in My Beer

Classic Country Song Titles

- "Alice Doesn't Love Here Anymore"
- "All My Ex's Live in Texas"
- "Bar Wars"
- "Before the Ring on Your Finger Turns Green"
- "Better Love Next Time"
- "Blues Plus Booze (Means I Lose)"
- "Breakin' In a Brand New Broken Heart"
- "Broken Promise Land"
- "Bubba Shot the Jukebox"
- "Cleopatra, Queen of Denial"
- "Cold and Lonely (Is the Forecast for Tonight)"
- "Come In Out of the Pain"
- "Cross My Broken Heart"
- "Does My Ring Hurt Your Finger"
- "Don't Come Home A Drinkin' (With Lovin' on Your Mind)"
- "Don't Your Mem'ry Ever Sleep at Night"
- "Down to My Last Broken Heart"
- "Drop Kick Me, Jesus (Through the Goal Posts of Life)"

- "Every Time You Go Outside I Hope It Rains"
- "Every Time You Throw Dirt on Her (You Lose a Little Ground)"
- "Excuse Me (I Think I've Got a Heartache)"
- "The First Word in Memory Is Me"
- "Fit to Be Tied Down"
- "Flushed from the Bathroom of My Heart"
- "For Rent (One Empty Heart)"
- "Friends in Low Places"
- "Get Your Biscuits in the Oven (And Your Buns in the Bed)"
- "Guess My Eyes Were Bigger Than My Heart"
- "Happy Birthday Dear Heartache"
- "He Left a Lot to Be Desired"
- "He's a Heartache (Looking for a Place to Happen)"
- "He's Back and I'm Blue"
- "Hearts Are Gonna Roll"
- "High Cost of Leaving"
- "How Come Your Dog Don't Bite Nobody But Me"

Carter's Barter

"If this doesn't put the 'cunt' back in 'country,' I don't know what will."

(**Carlene Carter**, on her husband-tradin' anthem, "Swap Meat Rag")

- "I Cheated Me Right Out of You"
- "I Forgot More than You'll Ever Know"
- "I Just Called to Say Goodbye Again"
- "I Just Started Hatin' Cheatin' Songs Today"
- "I Miss Behaving"
- "I See the Want To in Your Eyes"
- "I Still Hold Her Body (But I Think I've Lost Her Mind)"
- "If I Don't Love You (Grits Ain't Groceries)"
- "If I Said You Had a Beautiful Body (Would You Hold It Against Me?)"
- "If the Phone Doesn't Ring, It's Me"
- "If You're Gonna Do Me Wrong (Do It Right)"
- "If You're Gonna Walk, I'm Gonna Crawl"
- "I'll Never Forgive My Heart"
- "I'm Drinkin' Canada Dry"
- "I'm Gonna Hire a Wino to Decorate Our Home"
- "I'm into the Bottle (To Get You Out of My Mind)"
- "It Ain't Easy Bein' Easy"
- "I've Cried (The Blues Right Out of My Eyes)"
- "Jesus on the Radio (Daddy on the Phone)"
- "The Last Town I Painted"
- "The Last Word in Lonesome is Me"
- "Let's Do Something Cheap and Superficial"

- "A Million Light Beers Ago"
- "Mr. and Mississippi"
- "My Arms Stay Open All Night"
- "My Heart Has a Mind of Its Own"
- "My Past Is Present"
- "My Wife Thinks You're Dead"
- "My Woman Loves the Devil Out of Me"
- "Need a Little Time Off for Bad Behavior"
- "New Way (To Light Up an Old Flame)"
- "Not on Your Love"
- "Old Flames Have New Names"
- "Out of Sight and on My Mind"
- "Pick Me Up on Your Way Down"
- "The Power of Positive Drinkin'"
- "Pretend I Never Happened"
- "Queen of My Double-Wide Trailer"
- "Rebels Without a Clue"
- "The Right Left Hand"
- "Ring on Her Finger, Time on Her Hands"
- "Seven Days of Crying (Makes One Weak)"
- "She Feels Like a Brand New Man Tonight"
- "She Got the Goldmine (I Got the Shaft)"
- "She Left Love All Over Me"
- "She Met a Stranger, I Met a Train"

- "She's Actin' Single (I'm Drinkin' Doubles)"
- "She's Not Really Cheatin' (She's Just Gettin' Even)"
- "She's Playing Hard to Forget"
- "Should've Asked Her Faster"
- "Sleeping Single in a Double Bed"
- "Some Guys Have All the Love"
- "Stand on My Own Two Knees"
- "Stronger Than Dirt"
- "Tears Broke Out on Me"
- "Tears Will Be the Chaser for Your Wine"
- "These Lips Don't Know How to Say Goodbye"
- "They Ain't Makin' Jews Like Jesus Anymore"
- "This Romeo Ain't Got Julie Yet"
- "Three Six Packs, Two Arms, and a Jukebox"
- "Till I'm Too Old to Die Young"
- "Timber, I'm Falling in Love"
- "Too Many Hearts in the Fire"
- "Too Much Month at the End of the Money"
- "Too Old to Cut the Mustard"
- "Two Hearts Beat Better Than One"

- "Two of a Kind, Working on a Full House"
- "Walkin' Talkin' Cryin' Barely Beatin' Broken Heart"
- "Welcome Home to Nothing"
- "What Time Do You Have to Be Back to Heaven"
- "What's a Memory Like You (Doing in a Love Like This)"
- "Where Are You Spending Your Nights These Days"
- "Whoever Turned You On, Forgot to Turn You Off"
- "Why Don't You Haul Off and Love Me"
- "Why Have You Left the One You Left Me For"
- "Wishful Drinkin'"
- "Working Like the Devil (For the Lord)"
- "Y'all Come Back Saloon"
- "You Can't Roller Skate in a Buffalo Herd"
- "You Changed Everything About Me But My Name"
- "You Could've Heard a Heart Break"
- "Your Squaw's on the Warpath Tonight"
- "Your Wife's Been Cheatin' on Us Again"
- "You're a Hard Dog (To Keep Under the Porch)"
- "You're the Best Break this Old Heart Ever Had"
- "You're the Reason Our Kids Are Ugly"

Pickin' & Choosin'

> "I canceled my subscription to *Rolling Stone* the day they said, 'Three Dog Night takes Hoyt Axton's songs out of the realm of unfocused silliness and puts them in proper musical perspective so the masses can enjoy them.'"
> (Hoyt Axton)

Writing songs is one thing; choosing which of them to put on an album is quite another. It's a real challenge, according to **Doug Stone**—especially when you're desirous of broadening your hillbilly horizons. Having made a name for hisself by belting ballads, Stone was a little hesitant about veering away from his signature style to kick some booty with more boot-scootin' stuff: "It's real risky . . . because you're staking your career that they're going to like your up-tempos. But I figure, what the heck. I'm only here one time, and if I don't do it I'll turn around when I'm sixty years old and go, 'Dad gum, I wish I had done that just to see if they'd have liked it.'" Geez, how daring.

Alan Jackson has an easier way: He lets his pooch pick his performances for him. If the dog barks, the tune is a keeper; if he howls, it's a goner.

Stand By Your Man, Part One

This classic country tune is also one of the genre's more controversial works. A mini-feud was touched off by a comment **Hillary Clinton** made after learning her chubby hubby was in trouble—yet again. "I'm not sitting here like some little woman standing by my man like **Tammy Wynette**," she told the world defiantly, causing an outraged Tammy to demand—and receive—an apology from Mrs. Clinton (who has actually stood by her man through a lot more than most folks would).

My First Country Song

Every new artist is always on the lookout for that one "signature song," or "career record": a huge hit strongly identified with the perspicacious performer who first brings it to the public ear. One example is **Billy Ray Cyrus**'s profoundly unprofound line-dancing standard, "Achy Breaky Heart," which inexplicably propelled him into the stratosphere of superstardom. **Travis Tritt** didn't cotton to it near as much as the gazillions who bought it, though: "I think it degrades country music," he sniffed. "It says . . . what we're going to have to do in country music is get into an ass-wigglin' contest with one another." Yikes! The press had a field day with testy Tritt's critical commentary, touching off a bit of the old Hatfield and McCoy. "You really did it this time, brother!" crowed Tritt's best bud **Marty Stuart**. "You couldn't have opened a bigger can of worms if you'd said **Roy Acuff** was gay!" (Later in the year, BRC, while accepting an award for the ditty, pulled a coin from the pockets of his pantaloons and, parroting the title of Tritt's biggest hit, sniped, "Here's a quarter—call someone who cares.")

Country's Trademark Tunes

Roy Acuff: "Wabash Cannon Ball"

Lynn Anderson: "Rose Garden"

Bobby Bare: "Detroit City"

John Berry: "Your Love Amazes Me"

Clint Black: "Better Man"

Brooks & Dunn: "Brand New Man"

Tracy Byrd: "Holdin' Heaven"

Glen Campbell: "By the Time I Get to Phoenix"

I are smart

Deana Carter: "Did I Shave My Legs for This?"
Johnny Cash: "Folsom Prison Blues"
Patsy Cline: "Walkin' After Midnight"

"I hate it because it makes me feel like a prostitute. It's just a little ol' pop song."
(**Patsy Cline**, on her signature tune)

Diamond Rio: "Meet in the Middle"
Donna Fargo: "The Happiest Girl in the Whole U.S.A."
Merle Haggard: "Okie from Muskogee"
Faith Hill: "Wild One"
Waylon Jennings: "Luckenbach, Texas"
George Jones: "White Lightning"
Johnny Lee: "Lookin' for Love"
Neal McCoy: "Wink"
Mindy McCready: "Ten Thousand Angels"
Tim McGraw: "Indian Outlaw"
Jo Dee Messina: "Heads Carolina, Tails California"
John Michael Montgomery: "I Swear"
Willie Nelson: "Whiskey River"
Jeannie C. Riley: "Harper Valley PTA"
Marty Robbins: "El Paso"
George Strait: "All My Ex's Live in Texas"
Kitty Wells: "It Wasn't God Who Made Honky Tonk Angels"
Hank Williams: "Your Cheatin' Heart"
Tammy Wynette: "Stand By Your Man"

Stand By Your Man, Part Two

When asked to name the artist she thought had done the most vile version of her signature song, Miss Wynette said, "Tina Turner's was the worst. The range was unbelievably high, and I kept wondering how she was going to hit that high note. Well, she couldn't. I thought she did a horrible job."

Playing for Keeps

> "You go out and perform in front of live people, lookin' out at the faces, and it's real easy to come on and turn on. But in the studio it's just a bunch of old, ugly men."
> (Neal McCoy)

Before you can have a hit single, you have to go into the studio and record the darn thing, right? Many of Nashville's finest have logged hundreds of hours in recording studios, especially those that worked as demo-session thrushes-for-hire (like **Trisha Yearwood**) before becoming star songbirds themselves. **Deana Carter** says, "Burnt coffee, cigarette butts, and the smell of tape in a freezing cold room. That's what I'm comfortable with. That's home to me." Others aren't quite as relaxed. Nashville newbie **Wade Hayes** admits that, "[Recording] worries me sick. I don't relax. I drink a lot of coffee, and my hands shake a lot. I'm a bundle of nerves in the studio."

While Wade suffers from studio fright, **Mindy McCready** has a problem with stage fright. Before going on for her first industry showcase, she confides, all she could do was pray she wouldn't "hurl" in the middle of it. "I have no stage experience," she explained. "I'm scared to death. I sing so good in the shower, and then I get out on stage and I'm, like, quivering and fixin' to cry." With good reason, apparently. After a Texas concert, the *Dallas Morning News* noted her propensity for "smiling and waving at the crowd during sad songs," and called her "flimsy and shrill." The merciless reviewer also commented on her lack of authenticity and a "dance" she performed

Mindy McCready, back in the swim

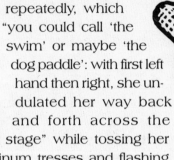

repeatedly, which "you could call 'the swim' or maybe 'the dog paddle': with first left hand then right, she undulated her way back and forth across the stage" while tossing her platinum tresses and flashing that nonauthentic smile.

"I wanna see your toe ring, Deana!"
What one fan yelled to **Deana Carter** at a concert

Travis Tritt confesses, "I sang at the World Series two years ago and I thought I was gonna have an *accident*. Everybody knows the lyrics to 'The Star Spangled Banner,' so if you miss the words they send you to Cuba."

Like **Loretta Lynn** before her, **Deana Carter** puts herself at ease by going sans shoes (her crew place rugs on the

stage to protect her beringed lower digits wherever she performs), explaining that "I have to kick those shoes off. I'm into this easy access, no sweat, barefoot realm." She also says she "didn't start the barefoot thing as a gimmick at all. It's like when you go visit somebody at their home and they answer the door in their stocking feet. You just naturally feel a little more, like, chill." Okay, dudette.

"People in hell want ice water, too!"
Deana's response to said fan

On the Road Again

"I thought [touring] was nothin' but just glamour—you get up there and you sing a few songs and that's it, and somebody waits on you hand and foot. I didn't dare think of ridin' two or three hundred miles with rollers in my hair, tryin' to sleep on the bus, and gettin' out at truck stops and eatin' hot dogs and hamburgers. That didn't enter my mind."
(Tammy Wynette)

The country club spends a whole lotta time on tour, some logging thousands of miles each month on the road. (**Ronnie Dunn** says, "I remember one day not long ago I came home from a long road trip and my three-year-old son asked my wife, 'Mommy, is he spending the night here tonight?'") It's a hallmark of hillbilly stardom which got goin' in large part because, before the days of record-breaking record sales, it was the only real way for country artists to bring in a decent dollar. (Performing regularly never hurts record sales, either—hello **Garth Brooks**.) Some end up being so at home on the road that they'd rather sleep in a bunk than in a regular bed. Plus, you can now trick out your luxury bus with the latest in gadgetry to make it look and feel like a five-star hotel. **LeAnn Rimes** has a unique vehicle, a Peterbilt front-end hauling a bus back-end. It has a TV for each passenger, a washer and dryer, and even a tanning bed.

"There's some other people in the business, I won't say who, who are on the road three hundred days. How ridiculous! They lose their childhood."
(**Lila McCann**'s dad)

> **"I don't want us to be just the proverbial shit-howdy show out there on the road."**
> **(Ronnie Dunn)**

Country shows have gone through just as dramatic a transformation as country music itself. Far from the on-stage simplicity of days of yore, when a lone crooner would step up to the mic without a lot of fanfare and warble along to his own gee-tar, to-day's showstopping spectaculars are akin to arena-rock pageants—they're filled with just as many outrageous antics, demolished instru-ments, and over-the-top pyrotechnics as any Ozzfest extravaganza.

Rocker wannabe **Garth Brooks** is the main man behind this new country custom, which not everyone cottons to. **Mark Chesnutt**, for example: "Like, sometimes people ask me to describe my stage shows. I tell 'em not to expect a lot of bells and whis-tles and smoke machines or to see somebody jumpin' around and hollerin' and climbin' ropes and smashin' guitars. Anybody can do all that and have a fancy stage set and get the crowd goin' while not even singing on key." But **Tracy Byrd** says he's get-ting with the times: "I'm doing things that if you'd asked me a year ago I wouldn't have had the guts to do onstage. Just moving around a whole lot more. Dancing a little bit. Wig-gling the butt just a tad or something like that." (Byrd, no shrinking violet, performed an entire concert atop a Nashville billboard after losing a bet to a disc jockey in January of 1997.)

Drive the new
SPITERO

Chet Akins, Make Me a Star

Before they became famous in their own right, many of country's hottest performers played in other people's bands—or their own. **Vince Gill**, for example, had his own bluegrass band for many years, and, after his marvelous musicianship (not to mention his matinee-idol looks) was noticed, he was offered a gig in **Dire Straits** ("Money for Nothing"), which he turned down. He also played on many a Nashville studio session, as did pro-to-the-bone thrush-for-hire **Trisha Yearwood**, whose dulcet tones were featured on so many demos that Music Row's powers-that-be started supposin' it might not be such a bad notion to give the girl a deal.

John Anderson played in a heavy metal band named the Weed Seeds.

T. Graham Brown had a soul band called Rack of Spam.

Roy Clark played in **Jimmy Dean**'s band—until the sausage king fired him for chronic lateness.

Ty England played guitar for **Garth Brooks**.

Vince Gill played in **Rodney Crowell**'s Cherry Bombs.

Lee Greenwood played sax for **Del Reeves**.

Wade Hayes was employed by **Johnny Lee** as his lead guitarist.

Waylon Jennings played guitar in **Buddy Holly**'s band, the Crickets (and narrowly escaped death in the plane crash that took the lives of Buddy and his band—see page 224).

Martina McBride sang in a rock band called The Penetrators ("I was so naïve. I thought, 'That sounds like a good name!' We'd ride around in this van with a hole in the bottom, eating sandwiches, and showing up to sing Pat Benatar songs.").

Lorrie Morgan sang with **George Jones**.

Willie Nelson played bass for **Ray Price**.

Lee Roy Parnell played in **Kinky Friedman**'s Texas Jewboys.

Johnny Paycheck played for legendary wild man **Faron Young**, who recalled, "I hired Johnny for about two years to work for me, but I never could make Johnny behave hisself. He was too wild. He was wilder than me. That's getting on with it, if you can outdo me. So I had to let Johnny go."

Webb Pierce's band, the Wandering Boys, included at various times **Faron Young**, the **Wilburn Brothers**, and **Floyd Cramer**.

Jason Sellers picked with **Billy Joe Royal** and **Ricky Skaggs**.

Ricky Skaggs and **Keith Whitley** both played in the legendary bluegrass band **Clinch Mountain Boys**. The leader of the group, **Ralph Stanley**, recalled that one time, "We were late for a show. I think we had a flat tire or something. I walked in and these two boys were singing the Stanley Brothers' music better than the Stanley Brothers."

Marty Stuart played mandolin for **Lester Flatt** and guitar for **Johnny Cash**.

Ernest Tubb's Texas Troubadours featured **Jack Greene** and **Cal Smith**.

Steve Wariner was discovered by **Dottie West**, who employed him as her bassist (he was only seventeen—Dottie did love them young men!).

Band of Gold

Country's All-Star Backup Bands

♪ George Strait: Ace in the Hole

♪ Hal Ketchum: The Alibis

♪ Kris Kristofferson: Band of Thieves

♪ Kenny Rogers: Bloodline

♪ Bill Monroe: Blue Grass Boys

♪ David Lee Murphy: The Blue Tick Hounds

♪ Charly McClain: Bluff City

♪ Hank Thompson: Brazos Valley Boys

♪ Buck Owens: The Buckaroos

♪ Ray Price: The Cherokee Cowboys

♪ Rodney Crowell: The Cherry Bombs

♪ Loretta Lynn: The Coal Miners

♪ Roy Acuff: Crazy Tennesseans, Tennessee Crackerjacks

♪ Barbara Mandrell: The Do-Rites

♪ Hank Williams: The Drifting Cowboys

♪ Toby Keith: Easy Money

♪ Lester Flatt and Earl Scruggs: The Foggy Mountain Boys

♪ Uncle Dave Macon: The Fruit Jar Drinkers

♪ Pee Wee King: The Golden West Cowboys

♪ Eddie Rabbitt: Hare Trigger

♪ Joe Diffie: Heartbreak Highway

♪ Emmylou Harris: The Hot Band

♪ Lee Roy Parnell: The Hot Links

♪ Gene Autry: The Log Cabin Boys

♪ Moe Bandy: The Mavericks

♪ Pam Tillis: The Mystic Biscuits (her mom would rattle on about her mystical experiences while baking biscuits in the morning)

♪ Bill Anderson: Po' Boys

♪ Doug Supernaw: The Possum-Eatin' Cowboys

♪ Lorrie Morgan: Slam Band

♪ Billy Ray Cyrus: Sly Dog (named his band after a one-eyed bull-dog he once owned)

♪ Garth Brooks: Stillwater

♪ Tom T. Hall: The Storytellers

♪ Merle Haggard: The Strangers

♪ Alan Jackson: The Strayhorns

♪ Kinky Friedman: The Texas Jewboys

♪ Ernest Tubb: The Texas Troubadours

♪ Jimmy Dean: The Texas Wildcats

♪ Porter Wagoner: The Wagonmasters

♪ Waylon Jennings: The Waylors

Fool Me Once

Yes, touring is repetitive. Yes, it's boring. And sometimes, especially if you don't partake of the "babe buffet" (see *Rock My World, Little Country Girl*, page 163) the only way to relieve the unrelenting dreariness is to blow off a little steam. **Ronnie Dunn** and **Kix Brooks** are notorious for their on-the-road high jinks—for example, they once dropped ten thousand Ping-Pong balls on their opening act during a show. But, according to Kix, "Our best [prank] might have been [on] **Jo Dee Messina**, who opened for us for a while. We kind of kidnapped her, you might say, and sent her up in a hot air ballon [Messina is afraid of heights]. She called us every name in the book." Some of B&D's tour-mates don't take this lying down. **David Lee Murphy**, having been pranked by the practical-joking pair, hired a "Macarena"-playing marching band to parade through the venue during Brooks & Dunn's half of the concert. Ronnie remembers the incident well: "It was in Washington, D.C. We were up onstage and all of a sudden this marching band comes down the aisle and starts playing right in front of us. We had to shut the whole show down for a few minutes until they quit."

Tracy Lawrence regularly pranks his tour-mates: He deposited five thousand live crickets in **Tracy Byrd**'s bus; set loose a bunch of baby chicks on stage while **Kenny Chesney** was performing; and loaded two greased pigs onto Chesney's tour bus. In retaliation, Chesney gave out Tracy's home phone number during a radio interview, causing Lawrence's phone-based security system, which was wired into the regular phone lines, to overload after a deluge of calls. Tracy got the final snicker, though—he changed his

answering machine message to a voice reading out a laundry list of Chesney's personal and business numbers. Heh heh.

George Jones, who once toured with **Buck Owens**, got a little miffed at Buck's egotistical insistence on being last on the bill. "'Now, Buck,' I used to tell him, 'you closed the show last night. Let me close tonight in this town, and you can close tomorrow night. We'll take turns, and that will be fair.' He wouldn't hear of it. . . . So I fixed him. . . . I was introduced, [and] was of course supposed to sing *my* songs, take an intermission, then let Buck come out as the final performer of the evening. It went exactly that way, except that when I was onstage, I didn't sing my songs. I sang only Buck's. . . . I didn't leave one song for him to sing." But the problem continued, so George did, too. "Another night, we played Charleston, South Carolina, with several other acts. Buck again insisted on closing the show. I put on some baggy Bermuda shorts and walked quietly to the back of the stage. Buck was lost in a tender ballad when I walked behind his band in those shorts. Only the audience could see me as I danced a jig. I looked like a banty rooster in bloomers, and no one onstage could figure out why the crowd was howling as Buck tried to sing his tune. Before Buck could look around, I was gone."

Junior Brown once donned a cow costume and danced on-

stage behind **John Michael Montgomery** as he sang his heart out to a sold-out concert hall. **Ricochet** (Heath, Greg, Eddie, Jeff, Junior, and Teddy) played a similar (albeit more elaborate) trick on **Rich McCready** and his band. Earlier in the day, the Ricochet-ers visited a local dime store, where they purchased costumes and ammunition. That night, they waltzed onstage during McCready's show, dressed in Indian head-dresses and sea-monster costumes, and shot up Rich and his band with Nerf bows-and-arrows and Silly String.

When **The Lynns** toured with **Jeff Carson**, they turned his portion of the show into a drive-by shooting—from a golf cart, with water guns . . . and not just once but twice! Well, Jeff fixed their little red wagons. At the end of the Lynns' show, they found themselves engulfed in smoke from the fog machines, courtesy of Carson and crew, who also then turned water pistols on the girls, prompting Patsy to flip her lid. "I'm gonna kill Peggy for starting this!" she yelled. "I should've worn waterproof makeup!"

Former tour manager **Phil Kaufman** was handling the band **Highway 101** during a particularly pranksome tour with **Randy Travis**. "The two bands got along real well," he recalls. "It had become a kind of tradition for the two bands to play a trick on each other at each gig. On the last day of the tour, [Travis's band] rigged **Cactus Moser**'s snare drum with flour and hung some filament wire from a beam onto his microphone. Cactus came out and as soon as he hit the drums the flour flew up in his face. When he started to sing, the mic kept moving away. . . . We would not let ourselves be outdone. . . . When Randy Travis came out and did his first song, right in the middle of it I rode across the stage on a bicycle . . . with a rose in my mouth; got off the bike, walked up to Randy, handed him the rose; got back on the bike and rode off the stage again."

I Ain't Got No Business Doing Business Today

> **"I've told millions of people in thousands of crowds that as long as the fans want to see me, I'll be on the road. That, and the fact that I haven't wisely managed my money, is why I'm still out there today."**
> **(George Jones)**

Different people deal with the stress of touring in different ways. Some get wrapped up in booze or hard drugs; some throw tantrums—and some just skip a date or two. **George Jones** is legendary in the country music world for a number of things, not the least of which is his past habit of missing more gigs than he played, leading to his notorious nickname, "No Show." George claims it wasn't really his fault, though—that a mess of malevolent mobsters were controlling his career, never even bothering to tell him about the shows he was supposed to be playing. "I know I missed a lot of dates on my own, but I wouldn't be scared to say that two thirds of the dates I missed I didn't even know about," he contends. George also says the mean ol' mob men would force him to do cocaine, then tape up his entire body so he wouldn't fall over onstage while performing. Boy, can Possum tell a story.

> **"I hope you all get heart attacks."**
> **(Jerry Lee Lewis**, to an unappreciative audience)

K. T. Oslin threw a major-league tantrum when she was preparing for a TV appearance and the water stopped running while she was

mid-shampoo. She slammed her makeup case to the floor, whacked her trailer door with as much force as she could muster, and screamed at a crew member. "I was ready to kill," she remembered. "If I had had a weapon, I would have used it."

And then there are the world-class talents of **Waylon Jennings** and **Johnny Cash**, who raised the level of stress-relief on tour to an absolute art form. In 1978, Waylon and his band trashed an entire hotel, tearing up four rooms plus a banquet room, emptying the ice machine onto the floor, and throwing sand into the air conditioners.

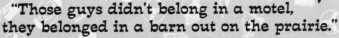

"Those guys didn't belong in a motel, they belonged in a barn out on the prairie."
(one hotel manager's reaction to the condition in which Waylon and his entourage left their rooms after checking out)

During **Johnny Cash**'s drinkin' 'n' druggin' days, he was pretty rough on the places he stayed. A couple of his more colorful pranks included the time he released a bunch of live chickens in a hotel elevator, and the time he flooded an entire building with a firehose. Another time, he and his band checked into a Minnesota hotel and decided to redecorate—by painting each of the four walls in Johnny's room a different (hideous) color in fast-drying paint: green, red, orange, and black. When a horrified maid confronted the naughty minstrels, they feigned innocence and magnanimously offered to stay in the room despite its rather unconventional look. The baffled worker left, and Johnny and crew got away clean. The band that plays together stays together, obviously—and when Johnny and his boys checked into a Georgia motel and found they hadn't been assigned adjoining rooms, they just made their own connecting entrances—by chopping holes through the walls!

4
Talk of the Town

Dirty Old Egg-Sucking Dog

Nashville is a big city but a small town ("this tiny village of country music," as **Lorrie Morgan** so disingenuously puts it), and, like small towns everywhere, it has its share of insider gossip. What do the stars (and the people behind them) have to say about one another when the thin veneer of civilization cracks?

Bitter in Babylon: Talent Agent Scott Faragher Speaks Out

Scott Faragher, a veteran talent agent, booked some of country's top names: the **Mandrells** and the **Statlers**, **Waylon**, **Tammy** 'n' **George**, and **Billy Ray Cyrus**, among others. In a rather bitter memoir (*Nashville Babylon*) of his crazy country years, Faragher weighed in with some behind-the-scenes ruminations on (and recriminations of) his famous charges:

MERLE HAGGARD

"... he was such a moron. In fact, everyone associated with him was an idiot. They all reminded me of the worst service station attendants."

MICKEY GILLEY

"... surrounded himself with yes-men and drinking buddies."

CHARLY McCLAIN

"... an opportunist ... overall bad attitude."

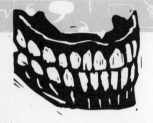

JOHNNY PAYCHECK

"The potential for lunacy always lurked beneath the surface. This could mean that he might get drunk and make an ass of himself, lose his false teeth, or anything else."

GEORGE JONES

"I did not have much use for George Jones as an artist or as a human being. He used to drive his car onto the steps of the Lavender-Blake building and hang around [the] office, wasting time and pretending to be drunker than he was."

RICKY SKAGGS

"He prided himself on being called 'Picky Ricky,' as if it was cute to be a jerk. He complained and whined about everything constantly. Complainers are bad enough, but the whiners are the worst of all, and Ricky Skaggs was a whiner."

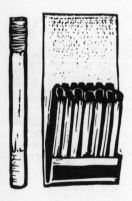

"He claimed to be very moral and refused to play anywhere alcohol was served. He was also opposed to tobacco, but when Marlboro started paying him twice what he was getting at other dates he managed to force himself to play for it, although his doing so was 'not an endorsement.'"

". . . greedy and unethical . . . he nauseated me, literally. . . . I still keep a copy of his checks around as well as a couple of photographs in the off chance that one day I might need some toilet paper."

Veteran tour manager **Phil Kaufman**, who went out on the road with Ricky several times, has a similarly low opinion of Skaggs:

> **"Ricky Skaggs played in Emmylou's band. He was just a little country bumpkin who didn't know shit from Shinola. To this day, his shoes still smell funny."**

Kaufman got a taste of Skaggs's intellectual prowess on a tour to Germany: **"I told him that the batteries in his Walkman wouldn't work in Germany because Europe was on different electricity. True to form, Ricky bought some new German batteries and gave me the old American ones to look after until we got back on American volts."**

Peer-to-Peer Network

It's not only the behind-the-scenes folks who have tidbits to share. Some of the best nuggets come from the people who are perhaps most qualified to critique country stars: other country stars.

KRIS KRISTOFFERSON

> **"Kris always wanted me to sing his demos—and with good reason."**
> (Mel Tillis)

PATTY LOVELESS

> **"There was no dehonkin' her."**
> (Liberty Records head **Jimmy Bowen**, referring to Patty's through-the-nose style of warbling)

LORETTA LYNN

> **"The kinds of songs [sister Loretta Lynn] sings don't suit me. . . . You have to be sort of hard to sing hardcore country."**
> (Crystal Gayle)

GARY MORRIS

"Gary was a cocky guy with a healthy ego who would tell fans to keep quiet during his ballads."
(Jimmy Bowen)

TANYA TUCKER

"Tanya? She still thinks asphalt is bowel trouble."
(Glen Campbell)

GARTH BROOKS

"I always refer to Garth Brooks as the anti-Hank."
(Kinky Friedman)

DOLLY PARTON

When Dolly decided to leave her mentor, **Porter Wagoner**, to develop a solo career, she left some very bad blood behind. Here's what ol' Porter had to say:

"Dolly's the kind of person that if you and I were sitting here with her and Johnny Carson and Huell Howser were sitting over there, and they've got a bigger [audience], she'll go over there. She would do that if it were her mother and her sister sitting here."

"Regardless of what it was or who it was—I mean, her own family, her own blood—she would turn her back on them to help herself."

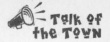

Life's Highway

You can take the hillbilly out of the country, but you can't take the homespun homilies out of the hillbilly. Drink down these sage little droplets of advice, and you'll never go astray.

How many clichés can you cram into one paragraph? **Joe Diffie** found out: **"To quote an old saying, you don't want to get off the horse you rode in on, but you don't want to travel over the same trail, either. It's always a little bit of a risk when you go out there a little bit and test the waters. But I just really wanted to try to take the next step."**

"It's not where you're going to wind up that is the most important thing. It's the journey you make along the way."
(Vince Gill)

"A mule's attention span is equal to roughly twice the length of the board you hit him with."
(Hank Williams, Jr.)

"Love should be simple, but it's not. Hate should be hard, but it's easy."
(Tanya Tucker)

"I've always said that life is like a blank canvas, and at the end you don't want to have nothing on it."
(Kathy Mattea)

"Pay close attention here. I'm going to reveal to you the three unmutable [sic], always-true laws of Honky-Tonk:
One: Eighty-nine percent of all bar fights are over women.
Two: Always make friends with the bouncer.
Three: No one can fight when you're playing 'Silent Night.'"
(Travis Tritt)

"You know, you got to make hay while the sun shines, man, because it can end tomorrow."
(Sammy Kershaw)

"If the watermelon falls off the truck, it ain't gonna get up by itself."
(Naomi Judd)

"If I had to trade one yesterday so I could have one more tomorrow, I don't think I'd do it."
(Garth Brooks)

"The rooster crows. But the hen delivers."
(The Dixie Chicks' old slogan. Their new one? "Chicks rule.")

"If you can't do it with feeling, don't."
(Patsy Cline)

"To me, the word *rules* was just something to rhyme with *fools.*"
(Merle Haggard)

"Excess in moderation. It's my motto."
(Lari White)

"When things are bad and getting worse, keep a cookie in your purse."
(Naomi Judd)

"The trouble with trouble is it starts out as fun!"
(Naomi Judd)

"A happy heart comes first, then the happy face."
(Shania Twain)

"Our journey isn't complete until we give thanks.
Let's be in the moment. Take a breath."
(Wynonna)

"The best place to find a helping hand
is at the end of your own arm."
(Naomi Judd)

"Y'all don't worry 'cause it ain't gonna be all right
nohow."
(Hank Williams)

"Don't give any shit, and put up with very little."
(Hank Williams, Jr.)

It's Hard to Be Humble

One thing country stars never lose is their humility, right? Um . . . not quite. These fine ladies and gentlemen aren't immune to the dreaded Hollywoodland ego disease—even if they couch their feelings in superficially self-effacing ways.

"I had a vision to make music—that music and my life could be used to bring something positive in this world."
(Billy Ray Cyrus)

"I'm starting to realize, getting older, that what really matters on this record is my gift . . . being an interpreter of my gift."
(Wynonna)

"I've been lucky, because with the instrument I've been given, I've been able to touch people with these songs that I've found very moving myself. Being a tenor, I'm able to connect directly to other people's hearts."
(Collin Raye)

"Only someone who has been there can appreciate the full-scale insanity that engulfs an entertainer with runaway popularity."
(Glen Campbell)

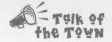
I Can't Be Myself

Rule Number One of Being a Big, Big Star: Talk about yourself in the third person.

"1998 will have more Garth music available than any other year in this decade—up to three or four projects."
(Garth Brooks)

"The workin' people in this country have supported Merle Haggard."
(Merle Haggard)

"You can get so caught up in being a 'star' that you can create an alter ego that is that star. I made a promise that if stardom ever did happen for me, I would not lose Mindy."
(Mindy McCready)

"Mindy McCready the Star."
(What Mindy McCready calls herself these days)

"I put on the outfit, the high heels, the makeup—and I become K. T. Oslin. She's a steamroller—nothing can stop that woman."
(K. T. Oslin)

"If it wasn't for Trisha [Yearwood] and her collection of hits package, the last time people would have heard Garth on the radio would have been over a year ago."
(Garth Brooks)

"I'm not supposed to announce this yet, but with the upcoming European tours we're going to try to start a world-peace movement. I want to make 1996 the Year of Peace."
(Garth Brooks)

"In 1971 I was invited by Queen Elizabeth II of England to the Royal Palace to sing. It was a command performance. There was a little flap in the press about a country singer sought by royalty. The combination, I guess, was unprecedented."
(Glen Campbell)
Like everything else about him.

"It went into the refrigerator hot liquid and came out a beautiful salad, full of wonderful fruit."
(Faith Hill, comparing her album *Faith* to Jell-O)

"There's gold in this here body."
(Tammy Wynette)

"You can't say you can't please all the people all
the time until you've tried."
(Garth Brooks)

"It ain't what you got, it's what you put out. And
boys, I can deliver."
(Uncle Dave Macon)

"I'm not in this business to make gold records. I'm
in this business to make platinum records. I ain't
near about through."
(Trace Adkins)

"I would drive up to the teller window at the bank,
and while I waited I'd sing along with Merle Haggard
or George Strait—whoever I was listening to. I didn't
know for six months that the ladies would turn up
the intercom so they could all listen to me sing."
(Tracy Byrd)

"Johnny Cash sent me a letter that said he was proud
of me for . . . walking with integrity and for always
giving thanks to the good lord. He said, 'I once had
a close friend that you remind me of.
He was Elvis Presley.' "
(Billy Ray Cyrus)

"[Legendary songwriter] Harlan Howard has become
one of my dearest and closest friends. . . . He said,
'I'm so proud of [your] record. I'm so proud that
you're carrying the flag for country music."
(Chely Wright)

Garthzilla

"I try not to let it get to my head. When they say I sold 129,000 albums in a week, it's like, 'This is cool.' If I did dwell on it, I'd be a pain."
(LeAnn Rimes)

Too late, LeAnn.

"Dad would say, 'Boy, nobody in the world can sing like George Jones.' And I'd think, 'Well, I can.'"
(Joe Diffie)

"I'm just a ramblin' guy with rangy hips. Of course I can do it all!"
(Kris Kristofferson)

"Although I haven't won the Entertainer of the Year award, one day I will."
(Neal McCoy)

"Incomparable. Way ahead of my time, bigger than Bob Dylan."
(David Allan Coe)

"If there is something I haven't achieved yet, I don't know what it is."
(John Anderson)

We can think of a few things . . .

"I get up in front of people and they call it entertaining. And I make too much money doing it."
(Garth Brooks)
I'll say.

"People used to ask me when Jessi [Colter, Jennings's wife] had her first big pop hit, 'How does it feel when she has a pop hit right out of the chute and you don't have one?' 'Well,' I says, 'being a goddamn legend, I don't really give a damn.'"
(Waylon Jennings)

"A legend is just another name for an old country act."
(Merle Haggard)

"I've seen audiences get tired of stars who are ten thousand times more talented than me."
(Garth again)
Agreed. At least about the "more talented" part.

"I done good."
(Mindy McCready)

"I think when people see themselves as the stars that other people do, it's pretty much over."
(Reba McEntire, who oughtta know**)**

Mindy the Mighty

"It's very advanced for what people are doing in country music in terms of content, style, and production."

(Mindy McCready, on her music. Unfortunately, Mindy's behavior doesn't seem to be quite as "advanced" as her music. Stardom really seems to have gone to her pretty little head—or maybe it's the Tinseltown influence, courtesy of former flame **Dean Cain**. In any case, her prima donna behavior and chronic lateness reportedly got her canned from her tour with **Tim McGraw**.**)**

I Am a Simple Man

Enough about me. What do you think about me?

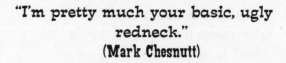

"I'm pretty much your basic, ugly redneck."
(Mark Chesnutt)

"I never did a little bit of anything."
(Waylon Jennings)

"I don't consider myself a hunk."
(Billy Ray Cyrus)

Neither do we, BRC.

"I don't have anything to hide . . . other than being a psychopathic ax murderer."
(Joe Diffie)

"I like to think of myself these days kind of like a butterfly."
(Ty Herndon)

. . . as in "Madame"?

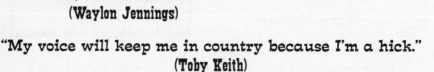

"I'm shy, I really am. . . . If I ain't got no rocks to kick and say, 'Aw shit,' I'm in trouble."
(Waylon Jennings)

"My voice will keep me in country because I'm a hick."
(Toby Keith)

"I know I can't change the world, but I know I can try."
(Reba McEntire)

He's a Good Ol' Boy

A Couple of Country's Larger-Than-Life Personalities

"Larry [Gatlin] will come in and ask, 'Would you like to see the top of my cowboy boots?' If somebody says yes, he'll drop his pants. . . . He'll drop his pants in front of strangers, stand there, and say, 'Aren't these boots pretty?' "
(Crook & Chase)

"Robert is crazy. I wish I were more like him, but I'm the logical one. He loves to make total strangers engage in conversation. I can't stand that. Last night we ate at a place called Joe's Crab, and the waitress asks for autographs. Robert scribbles on the menu, 'Thanks—this is the second time I've had the crabs.' I wanted to die."
(Trisha Yearwood on her husband, Mavericks bassist Robert Reynolds)

"I'm the toughest son-of-a-bitch that ever shat out of a mean ass."
(Jerry Lee Lewis)

"I'm not a media hound."
(Tim McGraw)

"If I hurt somebody's feelings, the burden I feel. . . . I don't like it. I love people. I'll do anything I can. I'd give my kidney."
(Jo Dee Messina)
No thanks.

"I'm just a bad ol' boy that made good."
(Randy Travis)

"I just consider myself your average Joe."
(Deana Carter)
Never seen anyone named Joe that looked quite like you, Deana.

"I never get tired of people telling me I'm not as big of a pain in the ass as they thought I was going to be."
(Travis Tritt)

"Sometimes I feel guilty because I'm not that interesting of a person."
(Joe Diffie)

"I don't look my age, so why should I act it?"
(Dottie West)

Yippi Cry Yi

Success, fame, money, power—celebs have it all, you say? Well, before you start thinking you'd like to try it, keep in mind that it's *just not as easy as you might think.*

"It's almost as if my job on this earth is to make other people smile, think, dance, laugh, cry. Sometimes it seems like singers and songwriters take emotions and turn them into a few moments of entertainment. It's a heavy load."
(Trace Adkins)

"It's a lonely business, bein' ballsy."
(Tanya Tucker)

"I'm just an emotional hurricane."
(Wynonna)

"I have to be one of the most misunderstood entertainers ever."
(Billy Ray Cyrus)

Or maybe he just misunderstood the word "entertainer."

"I don't like the word 'star,' but when you become one you attract press coverage, and the coverage isn't always honest or accurate. During the last twenty-five years I've become extremely distrustful of many newspapers, especially the tabloids. They lie so much, they have to hire somebody to call their dogs."
(Glen Campbell)

"Millions of people would have traded places with me, but not one of them could ease the loneliness I felt inside. They had no idea how hard it was being Glen Campbell, living in mental and spiritual bankruptcy."
(Glen Campbell)

"I think it's unfair to step off a stage after I've been singing my butt off and be met with two hundred people sticking pencils in my face. . . . The last thing I want to do [after a show] is sit there and hear from some little old lady from Indianapolis that Leroy didn't send the alimony check."
(**Larry Gatlin**)

"I'd been having hot flashes. I think the kind of life I was living—running, being pulled in different directions—worsened everything. Sometimes I felt like I was dying. I had to take stairs one at a time. I thought, 'I can hardly walk, and I'm barely fifty.'"
(**K. T. Oslin**)

"I've dealt with a lot of issues from childhood up to now, and I've become successful, and the pressures are great."
(**Ty Herndon**)

"I have been through so much in my life. I've had people die in my arms, I've been divorced, fired, slam-dunked, and shot at. . . . I have crawled over broken glass to get here."
(drama queen **Naomi Judd**)

". . . I wish when I get off the [tour] bus I could be more normal and go down to Kmart and buy me a fishing lure."
(**Alan Jackson**)

"Wal-Mart's probably one of the funnest places on the planet. I love to hit Wal-Mart, but I can't do it anymore. It's very difficult to go out."
(**Tracy Lawrence**)

"I'm a person that, if I love somebody or if I'm into something, I want to give it my all. And, more times than I'd like to remember, I got hurt from it."
(**Lorrie Morgan**)

"I've had some really rough relationships. I've been taken advantage of and walked on and hurt unnecessarily."
(**Jo Dee Messina**)

That's why she's a *country* singer.

"*When Food Is Love* by Geneen Roth helped me to understand that I have many years of healing to do. I was hungry as a child."
(**Wynonna**)

"I may be an eagle when I fly, but I'm a sparrow when it comes to feelings."
(**Dolly Parton**)

"Every time I get something fixed, something else falls apart."
(**Doug Stone**)

"There are times I feel like Charles Atlas [sic], with the world on my shoulders. Men think they're stronger, but they're not. And true men will admit to that."
(**Tanya Tucker**)

"Going from nowhere to platinum with the first album was like being hit by a tidal wave. And I used to try to calm myself by saying things will eventually get easier. But it [sic] doesn't."
(**Garth Brooks**)

Thinkin' Problem

Enlightenment reaches the men and women of country music.

"He had seen my mother and he thought, 'Now *that's* the kind of wife a man wants. Always there, good cook, good housekeeper, takes care of everything. Doesn't fuss and argue and all that kind of stuff.'"
(**Myra Lewis**, married to cousin **Jerry Lee Lewis** at age thirteen)

"[After we got married,] I didn't want to work and Clint didn't want me to work, so I didn't."
(**Lisa Hartman-Black**, spouse of Clint)

"She did what traditionally the wife does—sacrifice for the home and the family. I would have never asked her for that, but I wasn't above hinting."
(**Clint Black**, spouse of Lisa)

"If friends are over to the house watching football, she's in the kitchen making dips and chili and corn bread and all that kind of stuff."
(**Tim McGraw**, on wife **Faith Hill**)

"I don't like to cook. I think it's a woman's place to do the cooking. I'll go this far: I'll light the barbecue for my wife if she wants to fix steaks. When it gets right down to it, I can probably fix them better than she does, but I'd rather have her do it."
(**Glen Campbell**)

"I think that women have got it made if they know how to go about it. A woman don't have to work, really, if she don't want to and is smart enough to make a man a good wife—he's gonna take care of her."
(**Dolly Parton**)

"The wife I got back after my infidelity
was fifteen times the woman I had."
(Garth Brooks)
And with all that practice, he's probably *thirty*
times the man *she* had.

"I'm not telling anybody, 'If you're not
happy, go out and screw around because your
wife will become a dynamo for you.' I got to be honest
with you, that's what happened for me."
(Garth Brooks)

"I can't see any point in relating to a woman except sexually."
(Kinky Friedman)

"I've just seen the tops of their heads."
(David Allan Coe's comment on all the girls he's loved before. Coe
also used to wear a T-shirt reading "Damn near as big as Texas.")

"You know, the biggest hooker in the world is a housewife.
The only difference between a hooker and a housewife is the
hooker does *it* with a lot of people. A wife only hooks for you,
but she takes more money than a hooker would."
(Freddy Fender)

The Woman in Me

"No, I don't hate men."
(Mindy McCready's
response, when asked if she
was a feminist)

"I wouldn't call myself a feminist,
because I think that there are
differences between men and
women, and I believe in mutual
respect."
(Shania Twain)

"Sometimes I'll go to a radio
station and it's clear that the guy
has only heard my radio stuff
and not the rest of the album.
He'll look at me and say, 'Did you
write this?' And I'll say, 'Yeah.'
And he'll say, 'That's great, little
lady.' "
(Mary Chapin Carpenter)

"I've seen some of those guys in
Hollywood, those movie stars,
turn queer because they've done
had all the women they want."
(Faron Young)

The World According to Garth

"I came here thinking that country music needed me. I didn't dream there would be a million other people thinking the same thing."
(Garth Brooks)

Country stars can't forget that music is a business—and a certain "800-pound hillbilly gorilla" never has. Behind **Garth Brooks**'s unassuming, ultra-polite, regular-guy public persona lurks an ambitious, one-track mind sharply focused on getting ahead—waaaaay ahead. **Pam Lewis**, who used to share managerial duties with **"Major Bob" Doyle** ("We're a brand. We're a Campbell's soup or Budweiser beer."), says of her famous former client, "There's a lot of pretense and falseness and veneer. It's insidious."

"If there's a message in my life, in my career so far that I'm hoping people get, it's, 'If it can happen to me, it can happen to anybody.' I'm just not a fan of myself."
(Garth Brooks)

That makes two of us.

Nashville fixture **Ralph Emery** also has some choice words to say about the Garthster: "Brooks has always impressed me as a polite and well-mannered man, but I'm not sure if it's genuine or manufactured." And, alluding to the ease with which GB publicly cries on cue, "Brooks is in tears a lot."

> "I'm a control freak who wants to know what's going on every minute of the day because this is my one shot. It's not that I don't trust that they can't do their job; it's just that if I'm not going to do this for the rest of my life I want me to be the blame for that."
> **(Garth Brooks)**

From the very beginning, Brooks's britches have ridden mighty high, and he's micromanaged his own career, for better or for worse (usually, better for him and worse for everybody around him). Of course, when you're responsible for the lion's share of your label's sales, you can pretty much do as you damn well please . . . which he has. Former Liberty Records head **Jimmy Bowen**, a casualty in Garth's quest for glory, had a lot to say about his label's shining star in his Music Row tell-all, *Rough Mix:*

> "... he had yes-people everywhere else in his life and absolute control over everything."

> "Garth's image had suffered, I felt, when he and [wife] Sandy discussed his infidelity in a national magazine; when his eyes teared up on TV and he threatened to quit music; when he'd talk about all the pressure of his fame and wealth. No one was going to feel real sorry for Garth."

> "... Garth spent a half-million of his own dollars in January to advertise *The Chase.* He made his own commercial, but all it did was boast how he'd sold more records than anyone else. It made him sound like a carny barker. Our market research showed that the ad cost $70 per album sold while it ran. *What was he thinking?*"

As to the incident where Garth "outed" his sister (and bassist) **Betsy Smittle** during a television interview about his song "We Shall Be Free," Bowen says, "She had not come out on her own, and Garth had not cleared his remarks with her. He handled it poorly and showed his real colors in so doing. Their own family did not know. Her partner's family did not know. But now all of America did know."

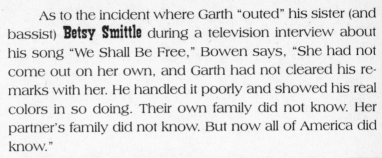

"We, including myself [sic], don't have faith that the EMI record label, after all the [staff] cuts, is firm enough right now to stand on its own and deliver a piece of product to other people."
(Garth Brooks)

Or even a piece of crap.

Garth didn't like Bowen, and he wasn't any more thrilled with Capitol Nashville head **Scott Hendricks** (famed for his fling with pre-Tim **Faith Hill**), whom Garth blamed for the relatively disappointing sales of *Fresh Horses*. (Dang me . . . only four million copies sold!) Someone had to go—and it wasn't gonna be Garth. He decided to withhold release of his album *Sevens*, citing his displeasure with the record company's marketing department, until the people he didn't like—including Hendricks—were axed.

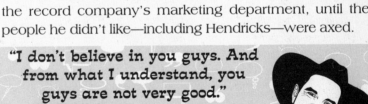

"I don't believe in you guys. And from what I understand, you guys are not very good."
(Garth Brooks, to Scott Hendricks and his crew)

"I'm sorry Garth was disappointed with the sales of *Fresh Horses*," Hendricks told *Newsweek*. "All of us would have loved to have seen sales beyond four million, particularly after executing a marketing plan that Garth and his associates signed off on." On record, GB denies having anything to do with the firings, calling the whole matter "senseless."

"... seven million, eight million ..."

"This label problem was all down to what I was supposed to do with the rest of my life."
(Garth Brooks)

With the new marketing team in place, Garth should've been good to go. Was he? Yeah, for about five seconds. When *Sevens*, released to coincide with the Christmas season in 1997, sold 900,000 copies in its first week out, Garth's comment was an offhand, "It's a start." But it didn't do quite as well as he wanted, so he made a Faustian arrangement with the queen of daytime television, cowslanderer **Oprah Winfrey**. He magnanimously offered to give seven days' worth of his earnings from the album to her Angel Network . . . with one catch—she'd have to plug the album on her show (we all know what that does for book sales). It went so well (the record went from selling less than 50,000 copies per week to more than double that) that he offered to donate all his earnings as long as his sales were more than 100,000 copies per week. Swell.

"It's been five years since I've felt a part of the industry."
(Garth Brooks)

None of these shenanigans have helped Brooks's reputation on Music Row, where he's feared rather than respected or admired. And he has (perhaps inadvertently) managed to clear out some other artists on his label who notice the Garth-centricity and bail. So far, casualties include **John Berry** and **Tanya Tucker**, who sued the record company for $50 million for damage to her career (the suit is pending). However, in his own defense, Garth says, "If the industry is going somewhere that Garth does not feel is right for Garth to go, then Garth has to stand up and say, 'Guys, I can't make that trip with you.'"

"Country music's still about honesty and sincerity."
(Garth Brooks)

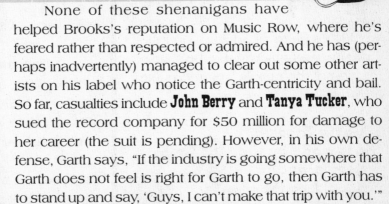

Oh, and money.

Play That Country Music, White Boy

On performing . . . party on, Garth.

"[The interaction is] like great sex where you get wild and frenzied, then turn that around quick to something gentle, tender, and slow, and then get wild and crazy again and just keep doing that over and over until one of you drops dead."

How Garth incites his fans: "You're winding the fat boy up! He's gonna go! He's gonna go!"

"They'll tear the building down if I tell them to. . . . That's when you're walking the line, and you're saying, 'My god, this thing could explode any minute,' but at the same time I want it! I mean, someone could get hurt! Wow! What a feeling!"

"We don't call 'em fans, we call 'em friends. Geez, I owe everything I got to God and these people." (Garth Brooks)

That's right, blame it on us.

Garth this, Garth that— why does he talk about himself in the third person? Well, let's let him tell us. "It's easier for me to talk about 'Garth' than say 'I,'" he explains. "'Garth' is supposedly the biggest-selling solo act in the United States. 'I' can't say 'I am. That feels egotistical to 'me,' and 'I' hate that feeling. Also, 'Garth' is what you see onstage. 'Garth' is the lighting rig, 'he's' the band, and most of all 'Garth Brooks' is the people out there. You gotta admit, 'the guy' would look pretty silly doing all that stuff if no one was reacting. So 'he's' just a reaction of the people." (Some quotes added.)

"Garth Brooks's life is made by the people, and it should be the people's." (Garth Brooks)

(And don't forget about www.garthstore.com Go there. Buy things.)

Kritics' Korner

⭐ *Garth Brooks* ⭐

"The Vanilla Ice of country music." (Rolling Stone)

". . . beady eyes . . . a circus clown." (Michael McCall, *Nashville Scene*)

". . . dispassionate and underwhelming . . ." (*Entertainment Weekly*)

". . . [his] big hat has become too small for his bigger head." (*Entertainment Weekly*)

"With a water bottle in each hand, he sprayed the crowd as he screeched the high notes (think Steven Tyler reeling from the constraints of extra-tight Spandex pants)." (*Dallas Morning News*)

5

Cashville, Tennessee

Bigger than the Beatles

"I couldn't believe it—to go from singing for a couple of hundred people to thousands. I could feel my heart beating in my arms. I raise my arms a lot when I sing and I could feel them just out of control."
(Mila Mason)

Ah, the sweet smell of success. You've paid your dues: you've worked a dozen menial jobs, eaten hundreds of boxes of macaroni and cheese, and sung on thousands of demos. Finally, your hard work pays off and you're the only one in the limelight. Is fame all it's cracked up to be? Hmm, let's think. Well, there's the money, of course. The fancy houses. The limos. The fact that you can now afford that new alternator. The adulation from your fans. And, of course, the money.

"I just never dreamed that all these guys would be standing at the front of the stage. It's so hard for me to put myself in that perspective. I'm going, 'It's just me. I'm a real dork, I promise. Really, you don't need to be fawning.'"
(Natalie Maines, Dixie Chicks)

While some stars act as if they're to the manor born, success affects a few of 'em a little differerently. Case in point: the Oak Ridge Boys' **William Lee Golden**. Once the Boys hit the top, he became obsessed with the "old ways" and took to sleeping on buffalo skins, wearing buckskin get-ups, and letting his hair grow to ZZ Top–like lengths. In addition, he installed tepees and a sweat lodge in his backyard. It all became a little too over the top for the rest of the Oaks, who ultimately replaced him with ill-fated **Steve Sanders**.

"Fame has its price, and the price is expensive."
(Glen Campbell)

"When you're fourteen or fifteen years old and you think about being a rock star or a country singer, the thing you think about is being out onstage in front of screaming fans, beautiful women and throwing your sweat around. That's what I always thought about and that's the impetus that drives my career."
(Tim McGraw)

" 'Celebrity' is an interesting thing. I think everybody who signs a deal should be whisked into some kind of camp so they can learn to protect themselves."
(Hal Ketchum)

"Success is having to worry about every darned thing in the world except money."
(Johnny Cash)

"[Fame] is like being in a public shithouse, and everybody's writing on the wall."
(Kris Kristofferson)

"The honor of being nominated used to be enough, but not anymore—I've got to be honest with you. To be nominated and not win and sit there after you have gotten a taste of winning—it really draws you up in a knot. It's time for someone else to win. I'm mature enough that I can handle that."
(Reba McEntire)

Yeah—sounds like it.

Rumor Has It

"I buy [*The National Enquirer*] every week and read it. And *love* to read it. Until I'm in it. And then I'm furious."
(Tammy Wynette)

The *Enquirer* also made the Hatchers—oops, I mean the Travises (Randy and Lib)—fighting mad when it ran an article about their alleged marriage of convenience. The piece claimed Randy was gay, having an in-name-only relationship with Lib. His reaction? "Yeah, I've heard that I'm supposed to have AIDS, that I'm supposed to be gay, that I'm supposed to be seeing Dolly Parton. You know, you try not to let that stuff bother you . . ."

"I'm tired of selling newspapers. I want to sell *records!*"
(Tanya Tucker)

We're Not the Jet Set

Can a country star have it all and still remain true to his or her blue-collar roots? You betcha—in fact, it's a source of pride to many. Even those who class up their acts at least pretend they haven't forgotten who they used to be (whether that's really the case or not), and they're anxious to prove they're the same ol' "just plain folks" they were before they became famous—even if they're now driving Ferraris instead of tractors and eating caviar instead of corn bread.

"People look at you and you can tell they're thinking 'He refuses to grow up and get a real job.'"
(John Michael Montgomery)

"The first time I got asked to do *Lifestyles of the Rich and Famous*, I cracked up laughing and refused to do it. Check my refrigerator for brie and see if you can get those Playmates out of the pool!"
(Travis Tritt)

"I still take out the trash at home, I promise. And clean up when the dog pees on the floor."
(Tracy Lawrence)

"I still like to pee off the porch every now and then. There's nothing like peeing on those snobs in Beverly Hills."
(Dolly Parton)

"When we was kids, we would always drink out of [tin cans]. It seems to keep things colder. Even at my beautiful homes, I'm always drinking out of a tin can, which drives my secretary nuts. I'm saving coffee cans to drink out of and she's throwing them out, and it makes me so mad."
(Dolly Parton)

Dang! That's Tasty!

About as "ritzy" as some stars get is openin' a box of crackers.

"I like meat and potatoes and corn
fritters with honey and butter on them."
(Mac Davis)

"I wouldn't call myself a chef, but I've
been cooking since I was about fourteen.
Brownie mixes, Chef Boy-Ar-Dee pizza,
that's stuff I can cook."
(Rhett Akins)

"I grew up in the Can Belt, where you threw
a can of green beans in a pan, added half a
stick of butter, and cooked on
high for an hour."
(Lee Roy Parnell)

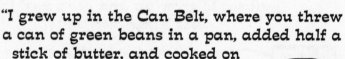

"I'd make gravy from fatback, milk, and
flour, pour it over two or three slices of
bread, eat the whole thing and go to bed."
(heart patient Doug Stone)

"I'd a lot rather have somebody brag on my
supper than my new record."
(Connie Smith)

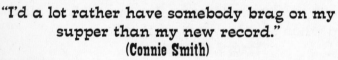

"My mother's a little embarrassed to
admit she likes to eat squirrel brains. But
back home it's a real delicacy. You put
the head in a pot of boiling water and
then crack it open with a spoon."
(Dwight Yoakam)

"I love gravy. Sausage gravy, biscuits,
and scrambled eggs. . . . I could eat
twenty-five eggs a week."
(Waylon Jennings)

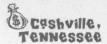

Pocket Full of Gold

> **"When people say less is more, I say more is more. Less is less. I want more."**
> **(Dolly Parton)**

"I've got more money than my children's grandchildren can ever spend," **Garth Brooks** brags. Indeed. *Forbes* estimated ol' Garth made $44 million in 1991–1992; in subsequent years his earning power was estimated to be $55 million per annum; and at the beginning of 1998, the pundits said he was worth about $400 million. Yee haw! That's more than **Dolly Parton**, who used to make about $350,000 (a week!) as a Vegas headliner, or **Willie Nelson** ($1.5 million per year from his Vegas dates alone), or **Kenny Rogers** (at one time, more than $20 million a year).

> **"When I think of the things I have, it makes me a little uneasy. I don't want people to think I've lost touch with reality."**
> **(Kenny Rogers)**

How does Mr. Rogers spend the spoils? Well, he bought an entire Hawaiian island, along with herds of high-bred horses, which he kept in "Cadillac style"—they lived the high life in a ninety-thousand-square-foot equine estate complete with tile showers and a heated pool. But great success doesn't come without great tribulation, according to Kenny: "I've got a custom-built Stutz, a Rolls, a Mercedes, a Ferrari, a Corvette, and a station wagon—but I've only got a three-car garage." Ah, the problems of being enormously wealthy (or is it "enormous and wealthy"?).

> **"Money is a way of gauging success. If I make more money, I'm doing more things right. If I make less, then I'm not doing as many things right."**
> **(Kenny Rogers)**

"I don't want to get rich, just live good!"
(Patsy Cline)

Feelthy reech **Barbara Mandrell**, the Aaron Spelling of Nashville, put her posh digs on the block in anticipation of moving to Tinseltown to pursue an acting career.
The largish (27,000-plus square feet) "log cabin" is quite a bargain at $7.25 million. You get three guest houses, thirteen bathrooms, fifteen bed-

rooms, a built-in fish tank, crystal chandeliers, a soda fountain, an indoor pool, a shooting range, and even a helipad. Hey, it could come in handy on those occasions when **Reba McEntire** drops by—she tried to get permission to construct a helicopter landing pad atop her gaudy Starstruck Entertainment building (home to her many companies and called "Taj MaReba" by the locals), but was shot down—figuratively—by the residents of Music Row, who were a little concerned that their recording studios weren't quite soundproof enough to handle constant chopper-blade action. Speaking of Reba, there's no end to how far folks will go to please her. Her record label, in appreciation of her coffer-filling efforts on their behalf, commissioned an artist to create a life-size bust of her son, Shelby. You just know one day we're gonna see that in a Reba museum.

"Never desire fame. Just the trappings."
(Kris Kristofferson)

Loretta Lynn, country's first female millionaire, owns the entire town where her big spread sits. Just outside of Nashville, **Alan Jackson**'s capacious dwelling is known as "Spendwood," and **Lib Hatcher** and **Randy Travis** live in a large log home on a lot of land crisscrossed by quaint rustic footpaths with even quainter names like "Travis Trails" and "Libby Lane."

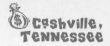

"I have all the material things I need and a couple I don't."
(**Willie Nelson**, who purchased an entire floor's worth of furniture from Sears when he hit it big)

Seems **Alan Jackson** has enough money to burn a wet mule—and he'll spend it on just about anything with a motor in it; he owns more than thirty-five cars and motorcycles, plus a Lear jet and a fleet of vintage boats. **George Jones** is also a speed freak. He recalls that, "I bought a Pontiac that [famed Western tailor] **Nudie** . . . converted. It was a white convertible, and there was a plastic dome to shield the interior. The dome was in the shape of a bubble top like those used by presidents seeking protection from assassins. (Mine wasn't bullet-proof.) Nudie embedded four thousand silver dollars in the dashboard, console, doors, and a part of the floor. The console was actually a saddle." Also, the door handles were guns and the horn mooed. Taste—you either have it or you don't.

Webb Pierce was well-known for blowing big wads on the same sorta thing. His 1962 Bonneville convertible also had six-shooters for door-handles; the brake pedal was a horseshoe; and a Western saddle was mounted between the two front seats. Strewn about the car's interior were silver dollars. You can see this shrine to excess today at Nashville's Country Music Hall of Fame and Museum. (Across the street at Spence Manor, you can also take a gander at one of the tasteful guitar-shaped pools Pierce built.)

Throne Rooms

Perhaps because a lot of 'em grew up without the luxury of indoor plumbing, country stars unfailingly have enough bathrooms around their green acres to make sure there's always a place to go.
Tammy Wynette had fifteen (plus, her doorbell chimed "Stand by Your Man"), and **Kenny Rogers's** huge Bel-Air (California) manse had six bedrooms, two kitchens . . . and thirteen bathrooms!

COUNTRY Confidential

Elvis Presley gave **T. G. Sheppard** a nicely tricked-out tour bus as a gift. T.G. vows to "always keep the bus. One guy wanted to put it up on blocks next to **Webb Pierce**'s swimming pool across from the Hall of Fame on Music Row and make a hot-dog stand out of it. Everybody wants to make a dollar off the man. . . ."

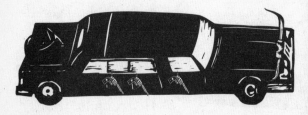

"Every material possession you acquire becomes a stick to beat you with."
(Rosanne Cash)

Waylon Jennings once decided he had to have a gold Cadillac—*right now*. Only problem was, he was on the road when the urge hit. No problemo—he and wife **Jessi Colter** trotted down to the nearest Caddie shack, where, according to Waylon, "Jessi stood next to me. I reached into her brassiere and pulled out a few hundreds. Then I pulled out a few more. I kept reaching and pulling until I paid the whole $45,000. Every now and then I'd pinch her and she'd squeal." (Who says romance is dead?)

"I started out even—it took me thirty years to get five million in debt."
(Merle Haggard)

Nuisance Tax

"I'm not worried about the next car payment, but I am worried about income taxes."
(Willie Nelson, before being nabbed by the IRS)

"I've been broke before and will be again. Heartbroke? That's serious. Lose a few bucks? That's not."

"Here was this guitar player from Abbott, Texas, who started out making eight dollars a day. How did he get $32 million into these guys? Somebody missed a stitch."
(Willie Nelson, after being nabbed by the IRS)

"With the first money I got, I built my parents a house back home, gave them a string of credit cards and said, 'Go!' "
(generous ol' **Glen Campbell**)

"My new prosperity allowed me to help my family financially. I built a new house for my mom and dad, and loaned or gave money to many of my brothers and sisters to start their own businesses. Many paid me back and some are still paying, but not one has ever stiffed me. I can't say the same thing about people outside my family."
(poor ol' **Glen Campbell**)

"I'm Garth Brooks after taxes."
(Little Jimmy Dickens)

Free Enterprise

"I love what I do so much that I'd do it for free if I could afford to."
(John Anderson)

"It's not that I have to be paid to do this."
(Chely Wright)

"Let me tell you, the acts that have been around for as long as we have and longer, they're not in it for the money. They're in it because they're doing something that they love."
(Marty Roe, Diamond Rio)

Country Boy, You Got Your Feet in L.A.

> **"When someone like me is approached to do television, it's usually to play a country-music star or a veterinarian who sings on the weekend or something."**
> **(Trisha Yearwood)**

What is it about stars from one genre wanting to leap boundaries and take up a completely different career as soon as they've hit it big? Dunno, but many country singers seem to have discovered their latent acting ability lately—maybe from all those high-concept music videos they do. Most of the time, these ill-advised flings with thespianism are turns for the worse. (Blessedly, it doesn't work in reverse—we don't see too many Hollywood stars cutting country albums.) **Steven Seagal** has evidently discovered how "hip" Nashville is—his schlocky flick *Fire Down Below* featured a star-studded roundup of country's leading lights, including **Randy Travis**, **Ed Bruce**, **Travis Tritt**, **Mark Collie** (**David Kersh** tried out for the part, but lost it to Collie), the **Lynns** (Patsy and Peggy, **Loretta**'s daughters), **Kris Kristofferson**, and **Marty Stuart**. (There *is* one big benefit to being in a Seagal picture, of course—anyone looks good acting next to him.) A recent episode of *Diagnosis Murder* also included a roundup of prominent country folk: **Terri Clark**, **Billy Dean** (he's also appeared on *Lois and Clark*, *One Life to Live*, and *Wings*), **Joe Diffie**, **Linda Davis**, and, in a leading role, the stunningly talented

Barbara Mandrell. And **Mindy McCready** is working on her very own sitcom, according to the rumor mill. That oughtta send the Nielsens through the roof.

> **"We do a certain amount of acting in our videos, and when you step off a bus after a twenty-six-hour ride to do a festival and you have to make it look like a party, that's acting."**
> (**Pam Tillis**, who's appeared on *Diagnosis Murder* and *Promised Land*)

There are two ways to go about learning one's craft: One can either plunge in and hope for the best, or one can do what drama queen **Tanya Tucker** did and get some professional help (some professional *acting* help). About signing up with the renowned Lee Strasberg Institute, she said she was "one out of four [accepted] out of seven hundred applicants. Celebrities have the hardest time getting in." (At least they knew she'd be able to pay.) Her sweat-of-the-forehead has paid off: She's appeared in *Hard Country*, *Jeremiah Johnson*, and *Georgia Peaches*. Stellar.

Rosanne Cash also studied with the Strasbergs. "The self-awareness was incredible," she gushes. "It was like being introduced to someone I didn't know: myself."

> **"I said, 'Should I take some acting lessons? I've never done this. I want to do a good job.' [Director Robert Altman] said, 'Nah. That'll just screw you up.'"**
> (**Lyle Lovett**, on the genesis of his acting career—which is actually going rather well)

Randy Travis had a teensy part in *The Rainmaker*, which has apparently convinced him he should be doing more board-treading. In fact, he says, "If **Steven Spielberg** came to me and said, 'I want to put you in a movie,' well, what do you think I'd do? I may not be a genius, but I can easily figure out the right answer to that question." Yeah. That'll happen.

"I never did know you had to be trained to have your picture made."
(Willie Nelson)

Some singing stars have indeed managed to make a second career out of treading the boards—like **Kenny Rogers**, whose stupid *Gambler* franchise lumbered on for quite a number of years, and **Dolly Parton**, who has a string of hits under her cinched-in belt: *9 to 5*, *The Best Little Whorehouse in Texas*, and *Steel Magnolias*. (Lest we forget, of course, she also made *Straight Talk* and *Rhinestone*. While filming the latter, costar **Sylvester Stallone** says he attended a party thrown by Miss Parton. "I showed up," Sly says, "and there were a lot of cowboy hats. . . . I said, 'Oh my god, I must be in the wrong joke, farmer.'") So can they really act? Well, Kenny plays himself, and Dolly is sorta charming. But neither are in the same league with **Dwight Yoakam**, whose seriously creepy performance in *Sling Blade* was a standout in 1997.

"This town does not own me. . . . If it gets to the point where I feel burdened or troubled or used in any way, Hollywood can kiss my ass."
(Dolly Parton)

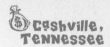

Tennessee Saturday Night

What's the difference between Nashville and L.A.?

"At the CMA Awards, six women shared a dressing room. You cannot have that in Hollywood."

(Actor/former Mindy fiancé **Dean Cain**, who probably won't be invited back to the famed awards show—at least until he reconciles with Miss McCready)

From the "Could We Possibly Be Any Luckier" department: A TV movie is being made from **Lorrie Morgan**'s autobiography (*Forever Yours, Faithfully*), the story of everyone she's slept with and all the bad things that have happened to her. Morgan says she admires fellow singer/thesp **Dolly Parton**'s career, but feels she wants to be "more of a serious actress. . . . I want to do very dramatic roles." (Your *life* is a dramatic role, honey.) Loopy **Loretta Lynn** seems to think the world needs a sequel to *Coal Miner's Daughter*, which "will be better. It will start from my first memory and it will go to my last thought." She'll play both her mother and herself in the new production, currently not on any studio's list of upcoming projects. **Barbara Mandrell** has given up country music entirely to focus on an acting career, and she too will have a movie made about her life. Her number-one draft choice for the starring role? **Jenny McCarthy**.

Sammy Kershaw appeared in *Fall Time* with **Stephen Baldwin** (the not-as-cute-or-talented Baldwin) and malodorous **Mickey Rourke**. But, Kershaw protests, "I don't want to do anything big. I don't want to be a movie star. Country music is where my heart is and where I want to stay." Sounds good to me. Stay. Aussie **Sherrié Austin**  appeared as a foreign-exchange student for a spell in *The Facts of Life* on teevee, and **Hoyt Axton** has appeared in several films, including *Gremlins* and *Heart Like a Wheel*. But he hastens to add, "I couldn't act my way out of a wet paper sack. When I saw myself on-screen in *Smoky*, I said, 'I don't want to do this.' I didn't act again for ten years." **Glen Campbell**, not usually known for his overarching sense of humility, allows that "I was so bad in *True Grit*, I made **John Wayne** look so good he won his first Oscar." (In fact, after seeing the movie one critic said he was "the ideal cowboy to chase a wooden Indian.")

LeAnn Rimes nixed a role in *The Horse Whisperer* because of "other commitments"—she's reportedly trying to arrange a multi-flick deal with Warner Bros. **Ricky Van Shelton** appeared on *Baywatch*, and thinks he'd "like to do some more acting if it comes my way." Let's see you in your swim trunks first, buddy. **Garth** knows just the kind of role he needs: "I'd want

to play something like a priest by day who, at night, turns into a psychopathic killer." Play what you know. **K. T. Oslin** goes one step further—she's willing to take her clothes off for the right picture: "I don't know where my movie career is going, if anywhere. I'm prepared to do anything, even nude scenes—but only with **Gene Hackman**, and with Mrs. Hackman far away."

Soaps seem to be a popular outlet for country singers' acting aspirations. Robotboy **Bryan White** appeared on *The Bold and the Beautiful* (does he fall into one of those categories?), **Tammy Wynette** was a regular on the short-lived *Capitol*, and **Reba** appeared on *One Life to Live*. The elfin Miss McEntire has also graced us with her charismatic characterizations in classics of the silver screen like *Tremors* and *North*, and she loved the Hollywood scene so much that she's looking for more projects. "I've got about five scripts that I like real well—two that we're really pursuing heavily," she says. She also has ambitions of winning an Oscar. One teensy hitch—she and hubby **Narvel Blackstock** only want roles that don't require her to change her down-home Okie twang. Gee, won't have to look real hard for those or anything. (As for Mr. White . . . well, we look forward to hearing his new album. Er, no we don't either.)

"I'm ready for my close-up, Mr. De Mille."

Clint Black and wife **Lisa Hartman-Black** starred together in the reeky *Still Holdin' On: The Story of
Cadillac Jack*, a 1998 made-for-the-tube
weeper about rodeo star Jack Favor, who
was convicted, and later cleared, of murder. Though Black's performance was
roundly savaged by the critics, his doting
mom has gone on record saying she thinks
he deserves an Emmy. Before she was a star,
Naomi Judd nabbed a part in **George Lucas**'s
American Graffiti—simply because he saw her
driving her vintage vehicle and wanted to use
it in the flick! Naomi also appeared in *Sisters*,
the TV drama in which daughter **Ashley** starred. (Taking nepotism just
a little too far there, girl.) **Mel Tillis**, on the other hand, is concentrating
on the writing side. He's already penned two scripts, one specifically
for the terminator, **Arnold Schwarzenegger**. "Arnold doesn't know it yet,
though," he admits. If Schwarzenegger's fortunate, it'll stay that way.

Act Naturally

More Hayseed Thesps

- **Bill Anderson:** semi-regular on the soap *One Life to Live*
- **John Anderson, Lee Roy Parnell, Mark Collie, Lila McCann, Collin Raye:** *Walker, Texas Ranger*
- **Johnny Cash:** *Gunfight* (with Kirk Douglas)
- **June Carter Cash:** *The Apostle*
- **David Allan Coe:** *Lady Grey*
- **Emmylou Harris:** *Baja Oklahoma; Honeysuckle Rose*
- **Mac Davis:** *North Dallas Forty*
- **Merle Haggard:** *Hillbillys* [sic] *in a Haunted House*
- **Naomi Judd:** *Rio Diablo*

- **Loretta Lynn** and **Porter Wagoner:** *Nashville Rebel*
- **Willie Nelson:** *The Electric Horseman; Barbarosa; Honeysuckle Rose*
- **Johnny Paycheck:** *Sweet Country Road*
- **Johnny Rodriguez:** *Nashville Girl*
- **George Strait:** *Pure Country*
- **Merle Travis:** *From Here to Eternity; Honky Tonk Man*
- **Randy Travis:** *Black Dog* (costarred in this Patrick Swayze stinker)
- **Travis Tritt:** *Rio Diablo; The Cowboy Way; Sgt. Bilko;* HBO's *Tales from the Crypt*

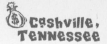

Born Believer

 "There was a time when music was my god. But since then, I've found a much better one."
(B. J. Thomas)

Strong religious beliefs are essential for country stars, who oftentimes live smack-dab in the middle of the Bible Belt. **Reba McEntire**, who *loves* to win awards, says God is her "Entertainer of the Year, every year." Ain't that sweet. **Skeeter Davis** refused to play clubs, those sin-drenched dens of secular iniquity, because, "If Jesus returned, and I know he will, I wouldn't want him to find me in a nightclub."

 "I pray every day that God will give me the strength, the wisdom, [and] the intelligence to use my career and the things he's blessed me with for good."
(Billy Ray Cyrus)

Wynonna believes in guardian angels, and admits to being obsessed with three things: Elvis, Mama, and Jesus. Wy's ma, **Naomi Judd**, who told every women's magazine in the country about her battle with hepatitis, is convinced she cured herself with a knockout combo of alternative medicine, positive thinking, and spirituality. Guess her doctors don't deserve any credit.

 "What I deserve and what I've gotten are totally off balance. Right now, if this world was split where part of 'em went to heaven and part of 'em went to hell, you'd probably be seeing me right on the front line of the people going to hell. All I can say is that [my success] is divine intervention."
(Garth Brooks)

We'd tend to agree.

Read Any Good Book Lately?

Dolly Parton consults the Bible whenever she needs to clear her head: "I'll either fast seven, fourteen, or twenty-one days. I don't drink nothing but water, and I don't ever say when I'm on a fast—scripture says you're not supposed to." (She does her fasting in multiples of seven days because of the great number of sevens in the Bible. Of course, there are also a great number of fives, eights, elevens, threes . . . oh, never mind.) Sevens play a big part in **Garth**'s life, too. When the time came in nineteen-ninety-**seven** to release his *Sevens* album, he just couldn't get over the coincidences (. . . or is it predestination?): "The album's coming out in the **seventh** year of a decade that's been tremendous to us. The pace that sales are going for us right now, orders of the album will probably take us into the **seventies** [cumulatively], as far as millions of albums sold. I was born on the **seventh** [of February] and the **seventh** letter of the alphabet, oddly enough, is G, so it's just time for all of that to line up." Whoo—uncanny.

> **"I'm so damned unlucky
> [that] if I died and got
> reincarnated, I'd
> probably come back
> as myself."**
> **(Freddy Fender)**

"Did you know that Nostradamus knew that the planet Pluto existed centuries before it was discovered by scientists?" asks **Merle Haggard**. Well, if we didn't, we do now. Thanks, Hag—and did you know you almost surely lived before? Just ask well-

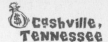

known psychic and reincarnation expert **Loretta Lynn**. "In one past life, I was a servant," she asserts, "bringing out platters of food to a bunch of men. And when the hypnotist asked me who my master was, I said, 'He's the king.' He asked me my master's name and I said that it was King George and that I was his girlfriend on the side—the queen didn't know about it. I told the hypnotist I lived near a village called Claridge and that I was very unhappy, because the king was going to be killed. Meanwhile, the king's best friend was grabbin' me

and making love to me behind the king's back, and I was afraid to tell the king about it because they were such buddies. Anyway, the king died before I did, and then his best friend choked me to death." That's sad.

      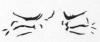

Lynn's mysterious powers aren't limited to seeing into her own past. "I look at someone's eyes and I know what has passed and I know what's comin'. I was about nineteen years old when I started feelin' this power comin' over me and I wondered what it was. People would say I was crazy if they knew the things that I do, but it's not crazy." No, of course not.

"I did a lot of bad things, got in fights with people, got divorced. All that stuff. My head was just pointed the wrong way, you know. Then I started to do a lot of reading. I got into [*The Prophet* author Kahlil] Gibran, got really into Edgar Cayce and his son, Hugh Cayce—books that had real positive attitudes." (Willie Nelson)

They Don't Make Love Like They Used To

Say I Do

**"True love is when you can walk around
your house without having to suck
in your gut."
(Marty Stuart)**

Ah, romance—safe to say it's country music's most popular theme. **Alan Jackson** (currently in the middle of one of those Let's-Divorce-No-Let's-Reconcile thangs) says of the woman who became his wife, "I remember one Valentine's Day when we started dating, I gave her a rear fender for her Volkswagen because the one she had was dented up. I thought that was pretty nice." (The lascivious **Lynn** sisters, Patsy and Peggy, think Alan's pretty nice too: Peggy says they'd love to tour with him, "But he'd never make it to the stage. We'd duct-tape him to the wall." Wow—kinky. Hope he doesn't have a lot of body hair.)

"The Ken and Barbie of country music."
(Alan Jackson, on the public's perception of
him and his wife, Denise**)**

Vince Gill recalls meeting his future wife, **Janis Gill**, "through music, and (we) were friends before we ever started hanging out—but when we first met, there was this little spark. I had a bigger spark than she did." The Gills, who seemed to have the ideal relationship, recently split. "My marriage is far from perfect," Janis told one interviewer, perhaps because "our egos and schedules get in the way." She also complained that she had to "follow him around the house with Dustbusters, one in each hand, cleaning up after him. He leaves dirty clothes, underwear, and socks everyplace." Gee whiz, girl, nobody's perfect!

"Hell, I'm only country."
(Jerry Lee Lewis's reaction to the public outcry over his marriage to Myra Gale, his thirteen-year-old cousin)

In the wacky proposals department, we have **Hal Ketchum**, who hid an engagement ring in a bunch of sunflowers he presented to his *cheri amor* as she stepped off an airplane. *Superman* hunk **Dean Cain** got down on his knees to propose to **Mindy McCready** and, not having a ring at the ready, laid a breadtie on her. "He went into this long mushy speech and then said, 'Will you marry me?'" she remembers. "I started crying. He took a green breadtie out of his wallet and wrapped the bread-tie around my finger." (Wonder if he demanded his bread-tie back after they split up.)

Reba's manager (now husband), **Narvel Blackstock**, one Christmas "had a bunch of big boxes under the tree for me. The first was an ice chest with a phone book in it, and on top of the phone book was a card that said, 'Try the other one.' The next had a note that said, 'Go to the next one.' So I went to this huge box, and it had smaller boxes inside, and finally I got a little ring box with this two-carat, pearshaped diamond engagement ring."

Love Out Loud

All-Star Country Couples

☀ Jason Sellers and Lee Ann Womack (in the process of getting divorced, perhaps because Jason says, "I love to be in love and flirt").

☀ Emily Seidel (Dixie Chicks) and Heath Wright (Ricochet)

☀ Faith Hill and Tim McGraw (she broke label chief Scott Hendricks's heart. . . . When she began seeing Tim, she was wearing an engagement ring given to her by Scott)

☀ Shania Twain is married to hardrockin' hitmaker Robert John "Mutt" Lange ("My husband made Billy Ocean's biggest album," she coos.)

☀ Deana Carter and songwriter Chris DiCroce

☀ Patty Loveless and producer Emory Gordy, Jr.

☀ Pam Tillis and songwriter Bob DiPiero ("Wink")

☀ Marty Stuart and Connie Smith

☀ Johnny Cash and June Carter

☀ Waylon Jennings and Jessi Colter (boy, has she put up with a lot)

☀ Amy Grant and *Prime Time Country* host Gary Chapman (now split)

☀ Clint Black and actress Lisa Hartman-Black

☀ Tracy Lawrence and former Dallas Cowboys cheerleader Stacie Drew (went through a very ugly divorce in 1997 . . . see page 178)

* Kitty Wells and Johnny Wright (celebrated their sixty-year anniversary in October of 1997)
* Rosanne Cash and Rodney Crowell
* Duane Eddy and Jessi Colter
* Vince Gill and Janis (nee Oliver) Gill
* Lorrie Morgan and Keith Whitley
* R. C. Bannon and Louise Mandrell
* Jeannie Seely and Hank Cochran
* Kris Kristofferson and Rita Coolidge (Apparently, the stress of keeping two careers going did this one in. He says, "I thought the marriage would last forever, but there was a competition there I wasn't aware of. I guess the pressures of keeping two artists not only under the same roof but also on the same stage are greater than I thought. There are some things you just can't make work.")
* Matraca Berg and the Nitty Gritty Dirt Band's Jeff Hanna
* Lari White and songwriter Chuck Cannon (he's divorced from Matraca Berg)
* Kathy Mattea and songwriter Jon Vezner
* Suzy Bogguss and songwriter Doug Crider
* Carlene Carter married both English rocker Nick Lowe and Howie Epstein of Tom Petty & the Heartbreakers
* Johnny Rodriguez and Willie Nelson's daughter, Lana
* Bluegrass babe Alison Krauss and Pat Bergeson (plays gee-tar for high-haired Lyle Lovett)

"Getting married is very special. I only want to do it once. Getting married is like—it's like meeting Elvis."
(Tanya Tucker)

And **Trace Adkins**, during his first appearance on *The Grand Ole Opry*, made his proposal to Rhonda Forlaw from the stage during a commercial break!

Travis Tritt serenaded his third bride, twenty-five-year-old Teresa Nelson (whom he met at a Hooters restaurant in Nashville—the chain is known for hiring waitresses whose measurements rival Dolly's) at their wedding with his song "More Than You'll Ever Know" (**Marty Stuart** was best man, and handed them their rings wrapped in jumbo-size scarlet panties—how tastefully romantic), and **Trace Adkins** crooned his tune "The Rest of Mine" at his wedding. But **Kenny Rogers**'s latest (probably not last) marriage was serenaded in a different way: by two very vocal animal-rights activists outside, protesting the inhumane treatment of chickens destined for the dinner table at Kenny Rogers Roasters "restaurants."

Hank Williams married Audrey (**Hank Jr.**'s mom) at a gas station. After they divorced, he wed his nineteen-year-old cousin, Billie Jean—not just once but three times (the latter two ceremonies being staged at a New Orleans auditorium for the benefit of paying customers . . . or rather, for the benefit of Hank). And **Trisha Yearwood** got hitched to Maverick **Robert Reynolds** (about whom she says, "I thought, 'This guy's too good to be true. He's gotta be an axe murderer, and I just don't know it yet.'") at Nashville's Ryman Auditorium.

> ## Lay It on the Line!
>
> "I'm not easily shocked, but **Patsy [Cline]** got to me one time. We were working in Canada and checking into a hotel. She looked around the lobby and saw this big Canadian Mountie. Right out loud she snapped, 'He's a big good-looking son of a bitch! I want him! I'm screwing the boots off him tonight!' And she took off across to him and did what she said she was going to do."
> **(Jimmy Dean)**

Lots of country stars like to be in love so much that they do it again . . . and again . . . ad nauseam. **Lorrie Morgan**'s first marriage (to **Ron Gaddis**, a musician in **George Jones**'s band) took place when she was just twenty. When that union dissolved, Lorrie moved on to **Keith Whitley**. After his death, she wed **Clint Black**'s bus driver, **Brad Thompson** (and had to pay him a big chunk of change plus a new truck in the divorce that followed). Lorrie laid off the marriage plans for a little while after that brutal breakup; she dated Dallas Cowboy **Troy Aikman** (who evidently likes country singers—he's also rumored to have romanced **Faith Hill**, among others), notorious womanizer **Kenny Rogers**, and local politico **Fred Thompson**. (That fling ended, she said, because, "I was feeling stifled at those political dinners and fund-raisers. I could not express myself as a pungent, pithy country singer." Ah yes—it's a drag to be prevented from being pungent.) Current husband **Jon Randall** is an aspiring entertainer who recently got a record deal—nothing to do with who he's married to, I'm sure.

It might be because of all this activity that Lorrie seems to have a bit of trouble keeping her stories straight. In her autobiography, *Forever Yours, Faithfully*, she compared herself and Keith to Romeo and Juliet, yet in a later interview with **Crook & Chase**, claimed Aikman was the true love of her life (she also told them she'd never had an affair with **Kenny Rogers**—something I wouldn't want to admit to either), and that the Aikman affair had ended because she wasn't a breeder anymore, having just had a hysterectomy.

After **Tammy Wynette** and **George Jones** split up, Tammy dated pro football player **Tom Neville**, **Rudy Gatlin**, and **Burt Reynolds** (who, she said, was hypoglycemic and nearly drowned in her bathtub once when he passed out). From Burt it was on to roguish would-be real-estate mogul **Michael Tomlin**, who stole a good bit of cash from her in their forty-four days of wedded bliss. "I made a lot of dumb mistakes," she admitted.

"We have a very beautiful but strange relationship. We don't worry about who the other dates."
(**Tammy Wynette**, on her relationship with Burt Reynolds)

Kenny, another of country's notorious serial daters, won over (now ex-) wife **Marianne**, a former *Hee Haw* cheesecake gal, by playing games—specifically her game, tennis. "It only cost me $10,000," he boasted. Of course, the divorce put him out just a tad bit more than that—$39,990,000 more, to be exact. What precipitated the split? One major reason may have been the sexual harassment charge filed against him by a trio of women who said he'd forced them to call his 800 number for kinky phone conversations (his way of having "safe sex," he claims—see page 197).

Gentle on My Mind

Glen Campbell has been more successful than most, but the heavily hairsprayed Stepford singer has also had more than his share of just plain unfair and downright dirty things happen to him. When *will* life give him a break?

Glen on ex-wife Billie Jean

"She would say, 'That song's not good' instead of 'That isn't the kind of song I like.'"

"I don't want to talk about Glen Campbell for his book. I don't even want my name in it. Put my name in it and I'll sue you."
(**Billie Jean**, when asked if she'd consent to being interviewed for Campbell's autobiography)

Glen on blond beauty Sarah Davis

(who was still married to Mac Davis when she began seeing Glen)

"Mac was my friend and still is as far as I'm concerned, although I can understand how he might be bitter."

"It's absolutely untrue I stole Sarah from Mac. They had split up before we started seeing each other. [Besides], we weren't that great friends. We just played golf together."

"Tragically, Sarah and I centered our life around cocaine."

"I'm not making excuses for what I did. My judgment and values were distorted because of the alcohol and cocaine."

"I didn't steal my best friend's wife. They were already apart, and anyway Mac and I were never friends."

Glen on Tanya Tucker

(who once said she'd "lay down her life" for him, heaven knows why)

"Tanya, in a way, was good for me in the first week of our relationship. . . . She spoke with compassion. I've since wondered if she wasn't simply taking advantage of a wounded man."

"I don't think she would have dated me had I not been a successful entertainer with access to a lot of press. She appeared to enjoy having her name publicly associated with mine. It's been suggested that she dated me to further her own stardom."

Tanya on Glen

"What he turned out to be was the man who could bring out all the bad in me, and I turned out to be the woman who could bring out all the bad in him."

It's a cryin' shame that **Glen** 'n' **Tanya** broke up before they had a chance to bring their glamorous, grandiose marriage plans to fruition. "We haven't decided where the ceremony will take place," Glen said at the time, going all gooey. "It could be on a 747. It's going to be a really big wedding. We even considered getting married on the first space shuttle—but that's a bit way out." Not for a big, big star like you, Glen!

"There were several false starts on my ending with Tanya. I couldn't get her out of my life as rapidly as I wanted because I was a weak creature of habit and manipulation."

Campbell's jealous streak was evidently a big cause of their frequent fighting. Cops were once called to a motel where Tucker was staying because big bad Glen was causing a big noisy ruckus. A sergeant called to the scene said,

"He was ranting and raving at these people trying to calm him down. He grabbed [Tucker's] guitar player by the shirt and we pried his hand away and told him to calm down or [he was] going to go to jail. He was yelling something about having his suitcase and keys in her room. She wouldn't let him back in there. He had a scratch over his eye— they had a fight or something. He said something to the effect that she had been with someone else."

"When we broke up, I felt as if I had been taken to the cleaners again by a woman, and couldn't help wondering if money had been her incentive all along."

(Glen Campbell)

"Glen didn't think I acted ladylike enough around the celebrities such as Milton Berle, Jack Lemmon, and Joe Namath and other rich people he liked."
(Tanya Tucker)

During their altercation-filled affair, Tanya alleges, she was seriously injured during one particularly ugly spat: "The fight raged on, and finally Glen reared back his arm and brought his elbow down in my face, shearing my two front teeth off right at the roots. I hit the floor, and all I could see on the carpet was blood. I reached my hand up and felt my mouth, and there was a gaping hole where my teeth should have been. . . . I asked Glen to take me to a doctor. He refused." Glen's response? "She's lying. She says I knocked her teeth out. I haven't even seen her in four years. She must need the money." (Later, she did file a $3 million lawsuit against him for verbal and physical abuse—which, she claimed, made her lose out on millions of dollars in show bookings while she was with him. The case was settled out of court, and neither party will talk about it.)

Tanya wasted no time jumping right back on the horse after she split with Glen, though—she dated a lengthy list of conquests (**Don Johnson**, **Dean Dillon**, **Andy Gibb**, quarterback **Jim Kelly**, and actor **Ben Thomas**).

"What I've learned from three marriages is to always fight fair, keep your punches up, never hit below the belt, and always make an argument end. Don't harbor grudges forever—and never resort to physical violence."
(Glen Campbell)

Why Baby Why

The Saga of George and Tammy

I Always Get Lucky with You

George Jones talks about the beginning of his relationship with **Tammy Wynette**

"I think there is something to be said for the fact that I went all over the country with a man's wife and never touched her until I had the decency to run off with her."

"Don [Chapel, her husband] sued for divorce, naturally, and he sued on the most serious grounds of all—adultery. I didn't think that was fair. Tammy wasn't wearing his ring the first time she and I made love. I had taken it off her personally."

Phantom of the Opry

George apparently had a teensy, troublesome jealous streak during his marriage to Tammy. Convinced she was having an affair with pompadour-pated **Porter Wagoner**, George confronted him in the Grand Ole Opry's men's room one evening. "**I walked up behind him and shouted, 'I want to see what Tammy's so proud of.' Then I reached around and grabbed his dick. I twisted hard. Porter began to jump and wave his arms. His sequin suit made him a blur of shimmering silver.**"

The Battle

Perhaps the most well-publicized incident in the stormy Wynette-Jones union is the one about a likkered-up George going on one of his trademark toots and shooting at Tammy.

She said: "... I heard a loud click, the sound of the safety on the gun being released. A cold chill ran over me. ... I turned just in time to see him raise the gun to his shoulder, aiming it directly at me. A loud blast echoed in my ears. ..."

He said: "Tammy claimed I fired a gun at her as she ran across our backyard. Nonsense."

After the shooting, she claims she heard George, higher than a Georgia pine, on a rampage inside their house, smashing furniture and breaking glass.

She said: "I went inside the house to look at the damage. When I saw what he'd done I sat down and wept."

He said: "Folks, it didn't happen." And, "[A friend of both Tammy's and George's] said he wondered if Tammy had ordered our staff to tear the place up so I would think I had made the mess."

Wynette then called the cops, who in turn called the men in the white coats.

She said: "He was dazed and out of his head when they put him into the back of the ambulance and drove off. I was so grateful the children were at school and spared the sight of their daddy squirming around in a straitjacket."

He said: "They put me in a straitjacket in the driveway of my dream home. ... Thank God the authorities didn't come on a concert day. No telling how many fans would have seen."

Can you say "stand by your man"?

If Drinkin' Don't Kill Me, Her Memory Will

"There's no love in the world
that can't be killed if you beat
it to death long enough."
(Tammy Wynette)

She said: "I said, 'George, every time you get drunk, you kill [our love] a little more. Every time you break a promise, something inside me dies. . . . Please don't kill the love I have for you.'"

He said: "She wrote that she knew I had a drinking problem when she met me in 1966. . . . A woman who married George Jones and complained that he drank would have been like a woman marrying the Reverend Billy Graham and complaining that he preached."

She said: ". . . he started turning the bottle up to his mouth and drinking it straight, which often made him gag. If he vomited, he'd turn the bottle up again and drink more. When he'd gone about six weeks without drawing a sober breath, I went to see his doctor alone. 'George is killing himself just as sure as if he'd taken a gun to his head,' I told him. 'What can I do to make him stop it?' We talked it over for a long time and decided that if George thought I was going to divorce him, it might shock him enough to straighten him up."

He said: "My gradual weaning from the bottle wasn't good enough for Tammy. She wanted me to be instantly sober forever. So she left me."

She said: "He nipped and I nagged."

D-I-V-O-R-C-E

He said: "I drank all day. I didn't want to go home in that shape. . . . I slept it off and called Tammy the next morning. I told her truthfully what I'd done, told her I was so glad I no longer did that routinely and that I'd be home in a little bit. 'No,' she said, 'you won't be at this house, you son of a bitch. Not in a little bit or not ever. Don't you ever come around me again.'
And she meant it."

Tammy had finally reached the conclusion that she could no longer tolerate George's unpredictability, unreliability, and constant drunkenness. She forbade him to come home—and stuck to her guns.

She said: "I didn't ask for alimony and I didn't ask for support for Tina, Jackie, and Gwen [Wynette's children with former husband Don Chapel], although I could have because he had legally adopted them. But I did ask for $1,000 per month child support for Georgette. (He made exactly one payment after our divorce was final. . . . I finally had to sue him for it.)"

He said: "The divorce was not complicated because I didn't contest it. I didn't even go to court. I told my lawyer to tell Tammy's that she could have whatever she wanted. She wanted most of what we had."

She said: "[I sent] word to George to decide what he wanted in the property settlement; then we could go from there. But George couldn't make up his mind."

Look Heart, No Hands

> "There were a lot of bad things—breaking and entering, trying to steal a van one time, trying to outrun the police quite a few times. There was a lot of drugs and alcohol use back then."
> (**Randy Travis**)

It's never a bad idea to hook up with someone who can help you professionally. **Randy Traywick** was a juvenile delinquent who was in danger of losing his freedom after a series of both petty and serious crimes (including car theft, drunk driving, and breaking and entering) when he met the woman who would change his life.

> "I can tell you the first dollar she got and how she got it. One day I was going down to my mother's house down a dirt road—there wasn't much blacktop then. She was probably two years old. I was holding her hand, and she said, 'Wait a minute, Daddy.' She saw a corner of that dollar bill sticking up on the side of the road. She saw the number '1' and the green. I think that's what got her started."
> (**Lib Hatcher**'s dad)

Randy met Elizabeth "Lib" Hatcher, almost twenty years his senior, at a talent show. She heard him sing, saw him perform, and was evidently impressed by his abilities—so much so that she attended Randy's hearing and persuaded the judge to release the young trouble-maker into her custody (Lib was married, but evidently ruled the roost—her husband didn't seem to mind having a young, handsome lodger in his house). Now, Lib's music-business experience was limited, to say the least—before buying a share in Country City USA (in Rock Hill, SC), where she ran into Randy, she'd been a restaurant worker, a clerk, and a ceramist. (When asked recently by one journalist when she'd started her pottery business, she summoned an employee into her lair and commanded, "Look underneath that flowerpot and see if there's a

Stand by your manager

date on it.") Soon, Randy (with a freshly minted last name), Lib, and her husband moved to Nashville. Lib took the reins at another club, the Nashville Palace, across from the Opryland complex, and put Randy to work both behind the scenes and in front of the mic. "Lib used to keep two coats for him," remembers former Nashville Palace owner John Hobbs. "A white one he cooked in and another one he sang in." Randy, in addition to working for Lib, had also moved in with her—and her husband.

> **"It was pretty awkward, living part-time with a woman and her husband who you weren't sure how he felt about you** [sic]**. Sometimes I wondered whether or not I'd wake up in the morning."**
> **(Randy Travis)**

Lib devoted herself to her discovery both professionally and personally, and somewhere along the line her marriage went belly up (though it was years before Lib and Randy confirmed the rumors that they were an item). Randy explained, "I think we discovered how much we needed each other. Her marriage had been bad, and I was a total wreck."

Through Lib's tireless efforts on her protégé's behalf, Randy began making headway in the country music biz—so much so that Lib opened a management office and hired a booking agent, Allen Whitcomb, to help keep up with the demand. She agreed to pay him a straight five-percent commission (low for the industry), but soon began to feel he was making too much money. To get her "revenge," Lib would wad up his paycheck and throw it at him.

Randy and Lib's union continues to be an interesting relationship, to say the least—rumors still fly about their alleged "sham" marriage, his sexual orientation, and her overweening interest in the long green. Perhaps booking agent **Scott Faragher**, an associate of Whitcomb's, has the best explanation:

> **"I believe that [Lib] married [Randy] not to stop the unfounded rumor that he was gay, but to keep him under control and to further confuse the financial picture so that if he ever split she would still come out on top."**

Rock My World Little Country Girl

> **"I said, 'You don't want to do that. I have an ex-wife you might want to call and confer with. I'm more trouble than I'm worth.'"**
> (**Marty Stuart**, response number one to marriage proposals from fans)

Fans: They can make life on the road worth living. Some of the more devoted bring gifts along with them (Spam-fan **Trace Adkins** gets tins of the stuff from his admirers; hot mama **Lorrie Morgan** gets bushels of one of her favorite comestibles, jalapeño peppers, from hers). Others make strange requests of their heroes. At one autograph session, **Clint Black** was approached by a nail-clipper-wielding woman. What did she want? Clint's clippings. (*Why* she wanted them is something else again—and we don't wanna know.) Laughs Clint, "I don't know what she could have wanted them for, but I had spent so much time gettin' them right, scrubbin' 'em and filin' 'em down [that] I just said, 'No, you can't have my fingernails.'" Another time, Black says, "one fan jumped on me and put her arms around my neck and her legs around my waist. And she wasn't no small woman, neither."

> **"Aw honey, I ain't nothin' but a worthless porch ornament."**
> (**Marty Stuart**, response number two to marriage proposals from fans)

After **Billy Ray Cyrus** hit the top of the charts with "Achy Breaky," he couldn't fight the goils off with a wet tow sack. A posse of fanatical females calling themselves the "Cheerleaders" followed him from town to

Willie and Waylon:

On the road again

town; so possessive of their lunkheaded hunk were they that they set his first wife's hair afire. (Luckily, someone had a pitcher of beer handy, with which they doused the blaze—whew!). Didn't take long for that divorce to become final.

 "Sometimes, at three a.m., there'll be a knock on the door and some females giggling. No one seems to understand that he needs some sleep."
(**Kenny**'s then-wife, **Marianne Rogers**, on touring with her famous hubby)

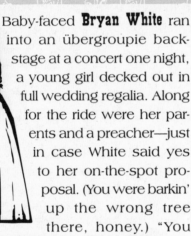

Baby-faced **Bryan White** ran into an übergroupie backstage at a concert one night, a young girl decked out in full wedding regalia. Along for the ride were her parents and a preacher—just in case White said yes to her on-the-spot proposal. (You were barkin' up the wrong tree there, honey.) "You can't date fans," explains **Travis Tritt**, "because fans look at you as larger than life. It's not a lot of fun to go out on a date with someone who's starin' at you like she's waiting for you to walk across the swimming pool." **Mindy McCready** concurs: "The whole time we're out, they're staring at me funny."

Love Can't Wait

Maybe **Bryan White** knows best when it comes to the dating scene. His philosphy: "It'll take your mind off of what you gotta do. You can't do that."

(Of course, "My mom says God will send me the right one, and he'll probably send her at the right time, too.")

 "I've met some nice girls on the road, but I run from one-nighters."
(**Mac Davis**)

All right, maybe it's hard for a star to get a regular date. But if there's one thing many male performers love about the road, it's the smorgasbord of warm, willing women who make each strange city a whole lot friendlier. These free 'n' easy lasses are variously labeled the "babe buffet," "slut puppies," and "bus toys" in the parlance of country, or, as **George Jones** observes: "The women, nameless beauties in every town, were as easy as a three-chord progression. Those who visited rock 'n' roll stars were called 'groupies.' Those who came to country shows were called 'snuff queens.' I don't know why." **Willie Nelson** admits, "You could say that they're what keeps a lot of us on the road so many years." (Nelson also confesses that, "I don't like to admit it, but if a girl baited her trap with sex, she'd catch me every time—and it's unlikely this will ever cease to work.")

Pay or Play

NO HEAD, NO BACKSTAGE PASS
(Slogan on David Allan Coe's road-crew T-shirts)

It's an unending source of temptation that proves too much for many. Good ol' boy **Travis Tritt** tells us about his bad-boy ways: "Let me define absolutely crazy for you: basically, sleep with anything that threw itself in my direction. I was young, twenty-seven years old. I was a rising country music singer. I was on the road. I had gorgeous women throwing themselves at me all the time . . . fantasy time!" And **Waylon Jennings** admits to servicing "two or three a night sometimes"— all stashed in different rooms of the same hotel!

> "The reason I got into this business in the first place was so I could drink whiskey, chase women, and have a good time."
> (Tom T. Hall)

I Don't Believe You've Met My Baby

Other side-effects of on-the-road carryings-on can have more long-term consequences, in the form of unplanned ankle-biters. Country stars who have been sued for paternity include Steve Earle, Billy Ray Cyrus (twice!), Joe Diffie (won't talk about it), and Kris Kristofferson (cleared of responsibility). Clint Black continues to pay support for a daughter fathered out of wedlock after a very short-term relationship with Renee Lynn Bain in 1989. Bitter Bain, who's never been exactly shy about telling the world about her tawdry dealings with Clint and co., was recently taken to court by him in a breach-of-contract complaint after she spilled her guts to a couple of sleazy tabloid reporters. A spokesman for Black said, "Clint's taking a stand against all gold diggers who try to get more and more money out of well-known people. She's damaging the child by speaking out." "They have trashed me, making me look like this terrible vicious person," Bain retorted. "This is not about me. This is about my daughter's future."

Don't Anyone Make Love at Home Anymore

**"It's a shame to say this, but the booze, the
wild life, the women, the stud that doesn't
want to settle down and take on
responsibility—that's all part
of country music."**
(George Jones)

The wanton wine-women-warbling lifestyle is just fine and dandy for single stars,
but it's all too easy for married
men to fall . . . and fall again.
Close encounters of the carnal
kind were the primary reason for the
breakup of **Doug Stone**'s first marriage, and
George Jones explains the reason *his* first marriage hit the shoals: "She suspected there
were other women, and there were. One-
night stands were a way of life for my friends
and me in those days. Shirley once caught
me in the backseat with a gal outside a Texas
honky-tonk." **Garth Brooks**, who's made a second career out of spilling his secrets to an
avid audience, says, "I just dove in and had
a blast. Beautiful women I thought were un-
real would walk up to me and say 'Sign this.'
Only there was nothing in their hands." GB was also offered $500 by
an audience member once . . . to let her perform oral sex on him. Ee-
yew!

**"I lost a girlfriend because I had to
work so much. My wife is kind of
happy about it, though."**
(Ray Stevens)

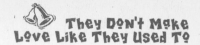

Ricky Van Shelton's wife, **Bettye** (love that extra "e," hon), details the oh-so-tough life of a country wife in her embarrassingly hokey confessional, *She Stays: How God Inspired a Friendship That Saved Bettye and Ricky Van Shelton's Marriage*, page after page of weeping, wailing, self-pity, and "inspirational" twaddle. According to the book, the sweet-as-Moon-Pie young fiancée of one of Ricky's associates took a special interest in dim-bulb Bettye and was her spiritual mentor through the difficult, heartwrenching time when randy Ricky was sowing his wild oats. (The more cynical among us might be forgiven for thinking that the young woman, an ambitious would-be country singer, had a little more than simple kindness in mind.) Shelton, though a self-confessed God-fearing Christian, had a tough time staying on the straight and narrow. Nashville talk-show host **Lorianne Crook** (of **Crook & Chase** fame) says he "told me of a time before he cleaned up his life when he awoke in his bus in a drunken fog and heard a girl in the sitting lounge yacking away. He said he walked out there and didn't know who she was. He didn't even know her name. He assumed he had picked her up in the bar where he had been the previous night. He couldn't even remember if he had sex with her. So he kicked her off the bus. He never did know what happened."

> **"I remember sitting there, looking at this girl whose name I didn't even know, and wondering, 'Why am I doing this?'"**
> **(Ricky Van Shelton)**

How easy is it to remain faithful when you're a top entertainer? Well, let's just say it's no piece of German chocolate. **Wynonna** confesses, "I'm in a very strange business. I have temptations and things happening to me all the time. Temptation! I can actually feel the darkness." (Maybe that's why she grimaces so much when she sings.)

Wild child **Carlene Carter**, who was married to English rocker **Nick Lowe**, reveals the struggle that comes with trying to keep a relationship together in this kind of environment. Before they wed, she says, "Nick had forgotten that he had asked me to come pick him up at this hotel. I got there, and this girl was sitting on his lap, and I knocked on the

window and I was dying inside, and he turned around. . . . I said, 'Get her out of there now!' and he said, 'Right.' He was scared. I made him cry he was so scared. So she left, and he cried, and then we got married." Even after they got hitched, though, things weren't exactly picture-perfect. "He's a rat (when he's on the road)," she said. "One time he told me what he had been doing on the road, and he kept saying, 'Come on, Cal, tell me what you've been doing.' I used to beat the shit out of him. I was so frustrated with hearing about it. I'm incredibly jealous that he's learned if he does do anything, he makes sure it's nobody I know. Because girls love to tell on each other." On the other hand, it's not exactly a one-way street: "I haven't been an angel, and Nick knows it. The thing is, you cannot live the way we do and not be tempted."

> **"Being married to an entertainer is like dog years: for every year of marriage, it must feel like seven."**
> **(Garth Brooks)**

Garth oughtta know—he found out the hard way what it takes to keep a marriage from hitting the shoals and breaking up. Before his career took off, the pudgy young Oklahoman met his wife-to-be, Sandy Mahl, at a nightclub where he was working as a bouncer. He'd been sent into the ladies' loo to break up a fight between Sandy and another quarrelsome gal— where he found his spunky future spouse with her fist stuck in a wall. ("Just wanted to scare her," Sandy explained. "I *meant* to hit the wall.")

They started seeing each other, and soon got hitched (one big thing they had in common was interest in his career). As Garth gained ground in the music business, he took full advantage of one of the benefits of his position: the bevy of beauties who are more than willing to assuage the loneliness of life on the road. Brooks was having the time of his lusty life—but life wasn't quite so peachy after long-suffering Sandy learned about

his on-the-road she-
nanigans. According
to **Lorianne Crook**,
Sandy "heard about
him looking out in the
audience, pointing, and saying, 'I want her, and then I want
her.'" She phoned her straying
spouse and, mad as hell, threatened to show him that
her boots were made for walkin'—walkin' out on him,
that is. That night, during his concert, Garth broke down
during "If Tomorrow Never Comes"; Crook explains,
"He says he began to cry right there, and out of the
crowd came a voice from someone who could not
have known about the phone call from Sandy earlier.
The voice rang out, 'Go on home to her, Garth!' Right
then and there, Garth said he got up, walked offstage,
and headed home to Sandy." "I don't know if I would
have stayed if the shoe was on the other foot," Garth says.
Aw, he doesn't mean that. "Yeah, I do know," he amends. "I would not
have stayed if the shoe was on the other foot."

> **"We're still fighting the war. We still have
> phone calls that end with one of us yelling,
> 'Well, it's over.' All the temptations are still
> there. I'm doing the best that I can with the
> second chance I've been given. But it's not**
> *Alice in Wonderland.*"
> **(Garth Brooks)**

Country spouses usually end up realizing there's
a certain amount of on-the-road shenanigans they're just gonna have to put up with.
But in certain cases, the sin is just too egre-
gious for even the most open-minded better half to forgive, much less forget. The
wife of **David Bellamy**, half of the **Bellamy
Brothers**, filed for divorce faster than a duck
after a june bug after she found a "groupie

catalog" in his briefcase. The book was filled with salacious snippets on David's fave-rave sexual partners (some of whom were underage), including addresses, phone numbers, nude photographs, and graphic descriptions of sexual preferences and prowess. (Bellamy also admitted to paying for a woman to tour with him, but protested that he didn't really know until later that "she followed **Kenny Rogers**, she followed **Alabama**—she's the biggest groupie in Hollywood.")

Gotta Have Faith

When **Faith Hill** went out on the road with **Alan Jackson**, rumor had it that music wasn't the only thing they were making. The alleged fooling around was denied by all parties, of course, one of the most vocal of which—curiously—was Alan's wife, Denise.

It's all too easy to fall in love with your co-performers, particularly when you're spending your lives together (on the road, anyway), and spouses of country stars may find it easier in the long run to "hold on loosely," in the immortal words of .38 Special. **Merle Haggard** claims his better half "always told me, 'I don't care what you do as long as you don't flaunt it in my face.' She realized that I was young and had a lot of things offered to me that I was not strong enough to refuse." That was a good thing, because when Merle and **Dolly Parton** went out on tour together, he fell for the considerable charms of one of country's biggest (no jokes, please) stars. "I didn't just fall in love with the image of Dolly Parton," he confesses. "Hell, I fell in love with that exceptional human being who lives beneath all that bunch of fluffy hair, fluttery eyelashes, and super boobs. And I was a fool to believe she loved me back." Hey, isn't she married? Well, yeah, but Dolly and her husband, **Carl Dean**, allegedly have a somewhat "open" union, where they are both free to have their dalliances but falling in love isn't allowed.

"Carl has wonderful relationships with other women, and by that I don't mean takin' them to bed. But even if he did—well, I'd feel bad, but the truth is it really don't matter. I think a lot of people run around who are happily married. You can't own the other person's emotions, and when you think you can, you have screwed up royally."
(Dolly Parton)

Is She or Isn't She?

"I have often said that I am closer to my friend Judy Ogle than I am to Carl, my husband, and it's true. . . . What would be the big deal if the rumor were true? There are a lot of gay people in the world. I'm just not one of 'em."
(Dolly Parton)

"He's not jealous and I'm not either," sez Dolly, who adds, "We're not trash. If I can't be with him, and somebody else can make him happy, fine. If he can't be with me, and somebody else can make me happy, fine." Alrighty, then. But the authors of *Poison Pen*, a tell-all about tabloid reporting, might not agree with your assessment, Dolly. "One summer," they wrote, "the *Star* had made a deal with a young boytoy (Blaise Tostie) of a prominent country-and-western singer (Dolly Parton) to tell all for $200,000, only to bury the story so as not to disturb negotiations between Parton and [Rupert, *Star*'s owner] Murdoch's Fox TV for Dolly's new variety show. Barry Levine, *Star*'s then bureau chief, and 'Big' Bill Dick, *Star*'s crazed news editor, had gone hog-wild on the story, treating Blaise like a mob witness being hunted by invisible legions of Gambino family gunmen. They hid him in a suite at the Four Seasons Hotel under a fake name. They hired a limo with blacked-out windows to ferry him from the hotel to the office."

"I have many wonderful relationships with men and women that are love affairs of a sort. I mean, sex and love are two different things."
(Dolly Parton)

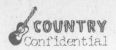
Feudin' and Fightin'

> ### "She was the kind of woman who was always under the thumb of the men in her life."
> ### (Tanya Tucker, on Dottie West)

Glam hick bombshell **Dottie West** had a propensity for knock-down-drag-out-filled relationships with younger men (especially the ones who worked for her . . . hopefully this category excludes **Steve Wariner**); she was forty-one when she married her twenty-nine-year-old drummer, **Byron Metcalf**. Not too long afterward, she filed for divorce, charging that "On several occasions, while under the influence of alcohol, he has caused embarrassing situations that are damaging to the plaintiff's professional career." Dottie didn't learn her lesson after ending that troubled tryst, though—she wed a twenty-eight-year-old ex-employee, Alan Winters, ten years later ("Alan will be a real incentive to stay young," she gushed). Sadly if predictably, they split too, amid a noxious cloud of allegations of cruel and inhuman punishment.

> ### "Nothing men do surprises me. I'm ready for them. I know how to whack below the belt."
> ### (Patsy Cline)

Willie Nelson and his first wife, Martha Matthews, had an unending series of vicious rows, which included her chasing him through a graveyard and throwing a fork at him so hard that it lodged in his chest (he wasn't seriously wounded). But the last straw came, according to Willie, when "I came

"I'm sure older guys are great lovers. But I just happen to like young guys."
(Dottie West)

home drunk, and while I was passed out, she sewed me up in a sheet. Must've taken her two hours. Then she got a broomstick and started beating the hell out of me. I woke up in this straitjacket, getting pounded like a short-order steak."

"The older I get, the more I wonder how we ever get together, men and women. We are totally different creatures."
(K. T. Oslin)

Merle Haggard says he and his first wife had just one really serious fight: "It started the day I met her and ended nine years, four kids, and countless external and internal scars later."

"A woman would have to love me a lot to put up with my bullshit," says **Johnny Lee**, and his high-strung sweetie, onetime *Dallas* doll **Charlene Tilton**, says she did. She accused him of beating her senseless ("trying to push my nose up into my brain") in front of their child, along with similar crimes of a similarly heinous nature. But Lee says they fought and eventually split because he just plain didn't cotton to her religious fanaticism. "I'm an old country boy," he explains. "I don't feel like I have to stick my arms in the air and wave and talk in tongues."

Tammy Wynette had a real problem with her first husband, **Don Chapel**—and no, the problem wasn't **George Jones**, at least not at first. It seems Chapel (who had an annoying habit of trading on Tammy's name to try and get his daughter a record deal) used to take nude pictures of his wife and trade them to other men with a similar interest in amateur photography. Wynette claimed she never knew what he did with the pornographic snaps until a "fan" walked up to her during a show and handed one of them to her. "It was a sickening, low-down thing to do," Wynette snarled. No wonder she left Chapel for the ol' Possum!

Take My Ring Off Your Finger

 "The biggest cause of divorce is marriage."
(Travis Tritt)

Trace Adkins and ex-wife **Julie Curtis** had a storm-tossed marriage that nearly end-ed in Trace's death. The story goes that in 1994 the temperamental twosome got into a heated argument over Trace's drinking and start-ed pushing each other around. Curtis reached for the phone, but Trace whacked it off the wall—so she reached for a gun. Adkins explains, "Being a macho guy like I am, I tried to scare it out of her hand. I said, 'Give me the gun, or I'm gonna take it away from you and beat your damn brains out with it.' I would never have done that, but I told her in hopes that it would scare her." Wrong move—she called his bluff and shot him straight through the heart. Trace was rushed to the emergency room, where he was revived, and the shooting was ruled accidental when he refused to press charges. Curtis hasn't exactly forgiven and forgotten: Now she's telling stories out of school about how he alleg-edly beat her. "People who know me know I wouldn't do that," he growls. "It's been uncomfortable, sure, but I don't run from my past. It's there for anybody who wants to see it."

 "I don't think there's ever been a friendly divorce."
(Merle Haggard)

After **Rosanne Cash** and **Rodney Crowell** split, they didn't speak—but continued their bitter battle by sniping at each other in their new songs. **Joe Diffie** was forced to do some writing of a different kind—during his divorce proceedings, he was required to

make a list of all the women he'd had sex with while he was still married. Gotta love that. And **Buck Owens** put *his* writing skills to the test after romancing (and dumping and romancing and dumping) **Jana Grief**, a member of his band. When they finally got hitched, it didn't take long for Grief to decide she'd had enough—after just two days of wedded bliss! This spurred brokenhearted Buck to place big ads in the local newspapers: "JANA JAE OWENS, I APOLOGIZE FOR BEING SUCH A FOOL. I LOVE YOU! BUCK" And "JANA JAE OWENS, I NEED YOU, MATT, AND KATHY [her two kids]! BUCK." Jana had to obtain a restraining order to stop the deluge of embarrassing public declarations.

> **"I always looked at marriage as something where you're married for two years and then you divorce."**
> **(K. T. Oslin)**

Former Dallas Cowboys cheerleader **Stacie Drew** and **Tracy Lawrence** went through an extremely acrimonious split just months after they married—sparked, she said, by a vicious argument that turned violent. After a September 1997 performance by Lawrence in Primm, Nevada, Tracy and Stacie got into a knock-down-drag-out fight over his gambling. During the brawl, Lawrence allegedly shoved her around, beat her, tossed her against a wall like a sack of potatoes, ripped out chunks of her hair, and threatened her life ("I'll kill you, you bitch!"). Stacie called the cops and had him arrested, but declined to press charges, claiming she didn't want the bad publicity. The district attorney *did* press charges, however, which made Lawrence's lawyer a little hot under the old bolo:

Is it possible she divorced him because of his fashion sense?

"I will go to court for him and enter a plea of not guilty, because that's what he is," he defiantly declared. "Then I will proceed to legally beat their brains in."

Lawrence filed for divorce about a week later, bitterly remarking that she'd just pushed him too far—that she'd repeatedly poked her finger into his chest and "cussed me like a dog." (Really great reasons for knocking someone around.) Lawrence's public declarations were a little more diplomatic: "We both tried hard, very hard, to make this relationship work, but at this point our lifestyles and goals are incompatible. Out of respect and love for her, it's time to move on." Stacie found these statements incredible. "While Tracy was telling the press he was acting out of love and respect for me," she said, "he was actually emptying our checking account, changing the locks on the house, cutting off my cell phone; (he) held my personal belongings hostage and kept my car." But, retorts Tracy, "If you have a dog and every time you walk past him you kick him, and then someday the dog bites back, is that the owner's fault or the dog's fault?" Discuss.

Lawrence was found guilty of misdemeanor domestic battery and fined $500, and confided to **Crook & Chase** that he was getting help for anger management. However, he added, "If one of us needs help, both of us need help." (In an interesting footnote to the split, Drew's dad later filed a lawsuit against Lawrence for recovery of the money he'd spent on their wedding, charging that his famous son-in-law had only married Stacie for the publicity value. In court papers, John Drew wrote that Tracy "encouraged Drew and the Drew family in their plans for the elaborate public wedding so that Lawrence would professionally benefit from the publicity given to the wedding by the Country and Western press.")

"I'm divorced and I've been to the
circus and seen the clowns.
This ain't my first rodeo."
(Naomi Judd)

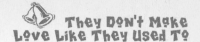
Oak Ridge Boy **Steve Sanders** and wife Janet Anne Sanders had a continuing series of violent altercations with Steve's ex, Mary Milborne Sanders, who said she felt that "Steve and Janet thrive on making me suffer." One particularly nasty quarrel took place between Janet and Mary in a grocery store, after a court ordered Steve to pay back child support (he'd also recently been handed a forty-eight-hour jail sentence plus eighty hours of community service when he was late in making a support payment). The pugilistic pair began a verbal duel at one end of the store, and by the time they got to the other end, fists were flying. The donnybrook ended with Janet bashing Mary's head into the floor, leading to Janet's arrest—and a burning legal question. One of the major topics of contention in the case was whether the floor could be considered a weapon, or whether the very definition of the word meant something had to be "picked up and wielded." (This is why judges get the big bucks.) In a motion to have the case dismissed, Janet's attorney wrote, "Ask the man on the street if a floor is a weapon and you would get incredulous stares," to which the prosecutor rebutted, "If Janet Sanders had continued to batter Mary Sanders's head into the floor it could have killed her." Janet was eventually acquitted, but the scandal forced Steve out of the Oaks.

7

STURM UND TWANG

Hello Trouble

What's a good country star without an arrest or two under his big-buckled belt?

In 1965, **Johnny Cash** was caught by customs agents at the El Paso airport with more than a thousand pills (at the time, he was ingesting more than a hundred per day) he'd picked up in nearby Juarez. He was booked for smuggling and concealing controlled substances. (Actually, "concealing" may be the wrong word: He'd rather haphazardly secreted the stash in his pockets and inside his guitars.) The following year, Cash was charged in Starkville, Mississippi with public drunkenness and thrown in the slammer, where he broke his toe trying to kick the walls down. "There's a lot of things blamed on me that never happened," says Johnny now. "But then, there's a lot of things I did that I never got caught at."

> **"I watch *Cops* regularly just to see if any of my relatives or band members are on it."**
> **(Travis Tritt)**

Habitual hell-raiser **David Allan Coe** was jailed in his teens for possession of obscene materials, car theft, and possession of burglary tools. While in the Ohio State prison, Coe bragged that he'd beaten to death an inmate who put the moves on him. Though he was sent to death row (interestingly, his father-in-law, also convicted of murder, later joined him there) for the crime, he escaped the electric chair when Ohio outlawed capital punishment. (Years later, Coe's tall tale was debunked by a television journalist.) About his time behind bars, Coe says, "I ain't goin' back to prison. Hell, I've gotten used to pussy and different things." (Colorful Coe is nothing if not a character—he has more than 300 tattoos, including a spider inked on . . . well, let's just say north of the knees and south of the sternum.)

In April of 1961, Western Swing star **Spade Cooley** bru-
tally beat his wife, Ella Mae Evans, to death—in front of
their teenage daughter. "Daddy stomped on her stom-
ach," the young girl told the authorities. "He sat me
down and said, 'You're going to watch me kill her.'" It
was a particularly brutal attack (Ella Mae sustained injuries—including cigarette burns and lacerations—too
numerous to list). At first, Cooley claimed she'd done
it to herself (in—depending on who he was telling his
story to—a car accident or a fall in the shower), but,
amid the overwhelming evidence, he was finally forced
to fess up: "I must have hurt her terrible. I felt horrible. I
was ashamed of her. I was ashamed of myself." He
was set off, he said, when she confessed to both
an affair with singing cowboy/famed straight-arrow
Roy Rogers and her desire to join a sex group ("Rock-
ets ran through my brain when Ella Mae told me of
her desire to join a free-love cult," Spade claimed). Cooley
was sentenced to life at Vacaville prison, where he died two months
before coming up for parole.

Merle Haggard, perhaps country's most famous
jailbird, was arrested as a teen for petty crimes
like car theft and kiting checks. But it was
a botched robbery attempt that
landed him in serious trouble—
and in the big house at San
Quentin (he was pardoned in 1972 by
Ronald Reagan), where he was inspired
to take up a musical career by seeing a
Johnny Cash performance. "Being behind bars was almost beginning to
be a way of life," he says. "I didn't
like it, but I didn't like life on the outside either." Eventually, the Hag
decided to get his act together. "I'm not sure it works that way very
often, but I'm one guy the prison system straightened out," he states.
"I know damned well I'm a better man because of it."

Ty Herndon spent more than a month in re-hab and was pinned with a thousand-dollar fine and five years parole after his notorious arrest at Gateway Park in Fort Worth in June of 1995. Ty's version of the incident was that he was simply out relieving himself (albeit unwittingly in an area of the park known for male prosti-tution) when *snap*—on went the hand-cuffs. Hmm . . . not quite that simple, ac-cording to the cops, who said Herndon was strolling alone through the park when an undercover vice cop spotted him. "What do you like to do?" the cop asked, whereupon Herndon freed willy and began masturbating. (Ironically, Herndon was scheduled to play for the Texas Police Associa-tion that very evening.) The officer arrested him for indecent exposure—then found two-and-a-half grams of crystal meth (speed) in his wallet. Uh-oh . . . big trou-ble. "I'll tell you what the moral of the story is," Herndon said bitterly after his ar-rest. "Don't pull off the road and take a leak in the woods, okay?" Okay. The incident had serious professional repercussions in addition to personal ones. Country stations dropped him from their playlists, citing their resentment of his hypocrisy—he'd long been known for paying sentimental lip service to those staples of coun-try culture, family and religion. The beleaguered singer began making public appearances in an attempt to salvage his career, begging his fans for forgiveness and support with the requisite tear in his eye. Now, Herndon says, he's glad the whole thing happened, because it forced him to stop doing drugs: "If I hadn't been arrested, I'd be dead by now."

Waylon Jennings was nabbed in 1977 after a cocaine-crammed parcel (marked "Confidential. Do not open"—always a terrific way to avert suspicion) addressed to him was opened by mistake in New York. The tipped-off cops, after logging its cargo, forwarded it to the singer, who was recording in Nashville at the time. A short

while after the package was delivered, police rapped on the door, intent on catching a country star with a boxful of contraband. But suspicious-minded Waylon and crew, sensing something was up, had flushed it all. Unfortunately, they'd forgotten to dispose of some wet plastic baggies, which tested positive for the drug, and Jennings was arrested and charged with possession and conspiracy to distribute. "Seems like the police would realize that the dealers of the stuff are not the hillbillies, you know?" Waylon snorted. "They arrested me on charges of 'distributing,' which is just crazy! Making the kind of money I make, why in the hell would I want to be in the cocaine-distributing business?"

George Jones has been arrested many times on myriad charges, including the attempted murder of his best friend, Peanut Montgomery, in 1978. The incident took place when a booze-addled George phoned his pal and asked him to drive down to the river for a chat. The men sat in their cars, and Montgomery, a recent convert to Christianity, began lecturing his buddy about the evils of intoxication. "I needed a friend, not judgment," Jones says. "'You don't know what I go through!' I [yelled], with my car window down. 'You need Jesus,' Peanut thundered, 'Repent! Repent!' 'Well, let's see if your God can save you now!' I said. I stared directly through the darkness into his eyes as I picked a pistol from off of the car seat." Peanut said George yanked a gun out, deliberately aimed it directly at him, and pulled the trigger. (Luckily, the bullet thunked into Peanut's car door instead of into Peanut himself.) No so, sez Jones: "I intentionally fired over his car roof. I'll believe that until my dying day."

Tracy Lawrence and his brother Stewart were just tooling along a Tennessee freeway minding their own damn business, they said, when a couple of unruly teenagers began making obscene gestures at them and then shot at them (cops called to the scene found no evidence of this). Macho man Tracy followed them all the way home, then pulled out a .357 Magnum and squeezed off a couple of shots—into the air, he said, as a warning. Not good enough, said the cops. Lawrence was arrested for reckless endangerment, firearm possession, and impersonating a police officer (he had a badge with him that said "Capt. Tracy Lawrence," along with an ID card from a phony police department). Lawrence blamed his "overreaction" on a mugging he'd endured a few years earlier (see page 203).

Willie Nelson was arrested for marijuana possession in 1994 in Hewitt, Texas, where cops found him asleep in his Mercedes on the side of the road with two ounces of pot in plain view on the seat beside him. The charges were later dropped (heck, he wasn't even driving!).

Johnny Paycheck exchanged harsh words with locals at a bar in Hillsboro, Ohio in 1985—reportedly over the merits of turtle meat versus deer meat (we've all wondered about *that*). Johnny got his gun and tried to settle the matter—by shooting one of his antagonists in the head. The bullet didn't kill the man, but Paycheck was arrested and imprisoned (he was sprung by fellow outlaws **George Jones** and **Merle Haggard**, who posted bail for him). "I was a victim of circumstances. It was an accident," Paycheck swore. Mm-hmm. This wasn't Johnny's first brush with the law—not by a long shot. While he was in the military, he spent two years in the stockade after being

convicted of assault; in 1968, he was arrest-
ed for burglarizing a house in Nashville; in
1971, he was arrested for kiting
checks; and in 1981, he was thrown
in the pokey again, this time for sexual
assault. The latter arrest resulted from an as-
signation with a female fan—he went home
with her after one of his concerts and stayed a
couple of days. Months later, she took him to
court for sexual assault of a minor, claiming that
while he'd been at her house he'd forced her twelve-year-old daughter
to have sex with him. (Paycheck's manager claimed, "He doesn't remember the facts or the situation or anything.") Why did it take the
woman so long to file charges? She "feared his power as a star," she
explained. Paycheck pled guilty to fourth-degree sexual assault, coughed up a thousand-dollar fine, and
was placed on probation. (He also settled a $3 million civil suit brought by the
woman.) Paycheck later theorized that the
whole thing had happened as a result of a
botched drug deal. Good one!

Johnny Rodriguez was arrested for
murder in August of 1998 after shooting a
man in Sabinal, Texas, the sleepy farming
town where he'd moved after his career
tanked. Here's what happened: Israel Borrego, who had partied with
Johnny on many an occasion, apparently entered
Rodriguez's house uninvited and in the dark of
the night, causing Johnny to mistake him for a
burglar. Rodriguez, who'd been across
the street at his brother's home, heard
noises coming from his own house and
went over to investigate. "It was dark,"
explained Johnny's attorney, Alan Brown.
"An intruder came toward him. He surprised
Johnny." Rodriguez didn't know who he'd shot
until it was too late, according to Brown. "Rodriguez did know him," he added. "(Israel) had

been coming uninvited. He had been told not to be in the house." Police arrved after Johnny called to report the shooting, and they picked up his .357 Magnum. He was held on a $250,000 bond and charged the following month with murder; at the time of this wrting, Rodriguez had not yet gone on trial.

Tanya Tucker's dad blew his stack after one of his daughter's gigs when he discovered some of the night's take was missing. Her tour manager had unwittingly scooped up some dough in order to pay the crew—an explanation that Beau Tucker didn't believe for an instant. He whipped out his trusty penknife and threatened the hapless man, who called the police and had his unruly employer thrown into the hoosegow.

Faron Young gave a good spanking to a very young audience member at one of his performances in 1972 (the bashful lass had apparently refused when he'd asked her to come up onstage with him). Her incensed parents filed a civil suit a year later, asking for $200,000 (although they ended up with just $3,400—before legal fees!). Young had also been arrested twice previously for drunk driving, and was also charged with physical abuse by two women he ran around with in the '80s.

Knoxville Courthouse Blues

Any star is gonna get sued—it's just part of the gig for anyone with a little fame and/or money. Many of the suits are frivolous, designed purely to lighten pockets rather than serve any real justice, but a few do have real merit. Herewith, a sampling of both types.

Garth Brooks was taken to court in 1997 by hip-hop star **Warren G** (and soon returned the favor by filing a countersuit), who objected to Garth's using a lowercase letter 'g' in his tour paraphernalia and marketing materials. (Oh please—like they have the same fans.) Garth blinked first, settling the matter by vowing he'd "strive to reach the standard that the 'g' represents" to Warren. "I learned from Warren G and Wron G, his manager, that the letter 'g' has a special significance to them and to some members of their community, in that it symbolizes kids and young people who have risen above the drugs and violence and who are worthy of respect because of their positive contributions to the world," blathered king-wuss Brooks.

While driving through a California wildlife preserve, **Johnny Cash** flipped a ciggie out his car window, starting a fire that burned more than five hundred acres of government property. The Feds hauled his butt into court, and he had to shell out $82,000 for damages and firefighting expenses.

John Conlee was taken to court by the American Federation of Musicians over allegations that he'd forced his band members to hand over their union-proscribed payments for playing the Opry. Conlee, according to hacked-off band members, had them on salary, and would deduct the fees he was required to remit to the AFM from their paychecks. Conlee's response? Well, he didn't feel he should be punished for the actions of his corporation.

In 1997, **Sammy Kershaw** filed a $2 million suit against a nightclub, the Super Toad Entertainment Center, for slander. Kershaw said he hadn't been paid before his show, as had been negotiated, so he just didn't go on. The manager of the club, who claims he has six witnesses, says he went out to Kershaw's tour bus to discuss the situation, whereupon Sammy pulled out a hogleg (according to the manager, it was "a big John Wayne–type gun") and threatened him with it. "I sued him for defamation of character and stuff like that. . . . I swear on my soul that I didn't pull a gun on nobody," Sammy maintains.

Loretta Lynn was sued by a black fan who said he'd suffered greatly after being humiliated at one of her performances. Caesar Gaiters claimed in his court action that she stopped her show in the middle of a song, pointed at him, and yelled out to the entire audience, "If you people don't know what coal looks like, here is somebody who knows what coal is all about. . . . Black is beautiful, ain't it honey?" The suit was later dismissed.

Never Go into Business with Kinfolks

◉ **Jimmy Dean** was sued by his brother, Don, who claimed he'd been grievously injured by remarks Jimmy had made about him (Don won, but the verdict was later overturned). Don had been an executive in Jimmy's meat company, and he said he'd been forced out. The sausage king's motive, according to Don, was that his country career was going down the toilet, and he couldn't handle the humiliation.

◉ **John Michael Montgomery** was sued by his stepmom, who reportedly wanted a share of the royalties for his song "I Miss You a Little," which JMM had penned for his dad.

Reba McEntire sued the Country Star restaurant chain when, she said, they refused to return items from her wardrobe that she'd lent them for display purposes. Like anyone would want to keep *her* wardrobe.

Barbara Mandrell lost a lot of admirers, not to mention the respect of the country cognoscenti, when she filed suit against a dead man, Mark White. Years earlier, she'd been involved in an auto accident in which White had swerved into her lane and hit her head-on. White was killed instantly, and Mandrell, seriously injured (her car's radio dials were embedded in her chest), had to be extricated from her smashed-up Jaguar. The suit, filed against his family, demanded $8 million in lost earnings, plus $25,000 for Babs's husband, Ken Dudney, "for the

Read Between the Lines
Taking the Tabs to Task

"People need to be shaken into reality, to understand these tabloids are not adult comic books. They are a mirror of America's shortsightedness, America's greed, and the emptiness of people's lives."
(Naomi Judd)

⚙ **Lorrie Morgan** sued *The Star* after it printed a story saying she'd had a wild necking session with **Bill Clinton** in the back of a limo. According to Ms. Morgan, "... I joined him onstage for the Christmas tree lighting in Washington, D.C. Other than that, everything else is totally fabricated and I take great umbrage with these allegations. I will be seeking legal recourse in this matter, and I will not tolerate such wild accusations which are so deliberately false. President Clinton has only been a complete gentleman in my presence, and I have never even met with him in a private situation." (Really, they ought to have known better—she's waaaaay too attractive for him!)

⚙ **Tammy Wynette** sued both *The Star* and the *National Enquirer* (who detailed fourteen surgeries and thirty-one hospitalizations in their article about the health of the frail star) in 1998 over allegations they made that she was a very sick lady—allegations which, she said, harmed her career because they implied she could "drop dead" any minute. The action was settled out of court.

⚙ **Loretta Lynn** filed a similar suit against the *Globe*—the paper alleged she'd had a drug overdose that left her "near death." "I've heard it enough and I'm sick of it," said Lynn disgustedly.

Stress Management

Many young country acts that become successful end up suing their first managers—often due to the fact that they know they can get a better deal once they've got some pull in the biz.

◉ **Mindy McCready** is a case in point: According to Quantum Management (who at one time employed McCready as their receptionist), she's declared bankruptcy to get out of her deal with them. The contract, which she signed when she was a callow lass of eighteen, called for 25 percent of her total income to go to them for up to nine years ("Unconscionable!" exclaims her lawyer). The folks at Quantum counter with the contention that her money burned a hole in her pocket, and that she was overspending—to the tune of $13,000 each month. ◉ **Tim McGraw** lost his bid to break his contract with original manager Carol Booth. Losing the suit means he's on the hook for $320,000, plus 15 percent of the dinero he's made since signing his record deal, as well as Booth's legal fees. (Good thing his wife works!) ◉ **Clint Black** fired his manager, Bill Ham, because "It was shocking to recently discover that the financial aspects of my business relationship with Mr. Ham were grossly one-sided and served to advance Mr. Ham's personal interest at my expense financially and professionally." Ham swears it ain't so, saying Black's claims are "a thinly disguised, self-serving attempt to escalate a business dispute and degrade it into a personal smear campaign." The disagreement started when Black decided to hire wife Lisa Hartman's mother, Jonni, a former publicist, to handle his career (prompting Music Row insiders to refer to Hartman as the "Robin Givens of Nashville")—and to replace Ham.

loss of the services, companionship, consortium, and society of his wife." The suit was settled out of court.

Johnny Paycheck was sued by a Frontier Airlines stewardess in 1981 after his abusive behavior on an airplane forced the cancellation of a flight—before they'd even gotten off the ground! The beleaguered stew had the pilots stop the plane so she could boot Johnny and a pal off the jet. The heinous offense? "Physical contact with a flight attendant and indecent language."

LeAnn Rimes was taken to court by a trio of ticked-off jingle-writers who claimed her hit "Put a Little Holiday in Your Heart" (along with her similarly titled, emptily sentimental Christmas novel and coordinating television special) was directly ripped off from a spot they'd written for Target store ads on which Rimes had been tapped to warble.

Kenny Rogers Roasters is the corpulent crooner's chain of fast-food chicken franchises. The "restaurants" have been taken to court a couple of times. First, they were sued by Cluckers Wood Roasted Chicken, which claimed Kenny had ripped off their menus and recipes. (A Cluckers attorney said, "He could be John Smith as far as we're concerned. But Kenny Rogers has personally gone out of his way to vouch for the Roasters restaurants, his name is out front, and his high level of notoriety cannot be denied.") In another lawsuit, this time brought by Roasters, a New York judge ruled in favor of a man who'd placed a sign in the window of his office, located above a KRR eatery. What did the sign say? "Bad food." In his decision, the judge wrote, "Were [he] to stand outside Roasters, physically approach and scream at customers that they would suffer from abdominal distension after eating Roasters' food, the balance may be tipped more favorably to Roaster." The ornery hombre claimed he was merely stating his own opinion about the chow, which was, he said, "overly salty, greasy, and [having] poor taste, consistency, and color." Sorta like Kenny himself.

Wynonna and husband Arch Kelley* wound up in a scandalous court case when a disgruntled ex-employee, Andria Surles, filed a discrimination and sexual-harassment lawsuit (which seems to have been settled, somehow . . . the case dropped off the media radar not long before the final judgment was to be made). She demanded $800,000 for various alleged offenses, including:

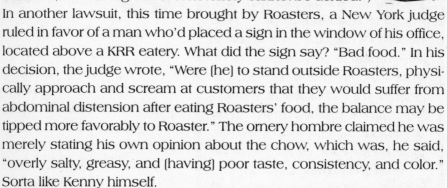

☀ Wynonna telling Andria she had a "cute butt"
☀ Wynonna asking for a massage—of her more than ample buttocks
☀ Arch's leering description of himself as "well-endowed"
☀ Arch's attempts to measure Andria's rear end with a tape measure

Surles also claimed she hadn't been paid as much as male employees. Well, maybe *they* played along.

*(*Is it true love between Wy and Arch? Well, maybe, maybe not. When asked by a friend if he and Wynonna were planning to get hitched, Arch Kelley replied, "Well, she's going to gross about ten million dollars next year. So what do you think?")*

Trouble on the Line

Noli me tangere

Bloated balladeer **Kenny Rogers** was sued in 1993 by two women who claimed he'd sexually harassed them by insisting they call his 800 number and talk dirty to him. (He claims they called the number of their own free will, and even had to enter a PIN number given especially to them.) Unfortunately for Rogers, the women made tapes of the conversations. Some highlights of Kenny's spiel:

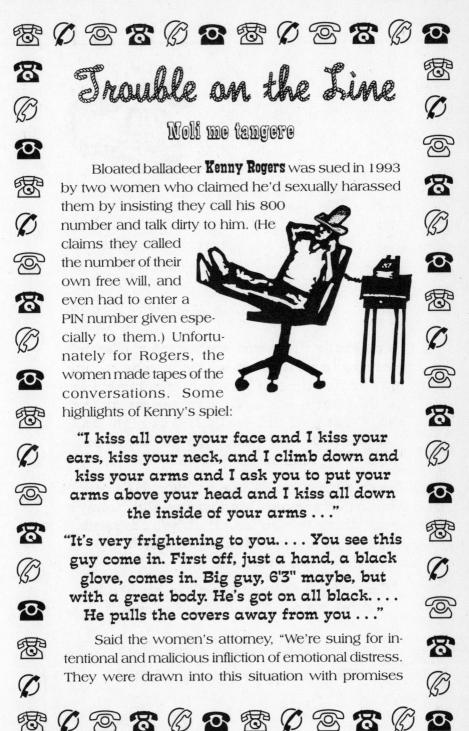

"I kiss all over your face and I kiss your ears, kiss your neck, and I climb down and kiss your arms and I ask you to put your arms above your head and I kiss all down the inside of your arms . . ."

"It's very frightening to you. . . . You see this guy come in. First off, just a hand, a black glove, comes in. Big guy, 6'3" maybe, but with a great body. He's got on all black. . . . He pulls the covers away from you . . ."

Said the women's attorney, "We're suing for intentional and malicious infliction of emotional distress. They were drawn into this situation with promises

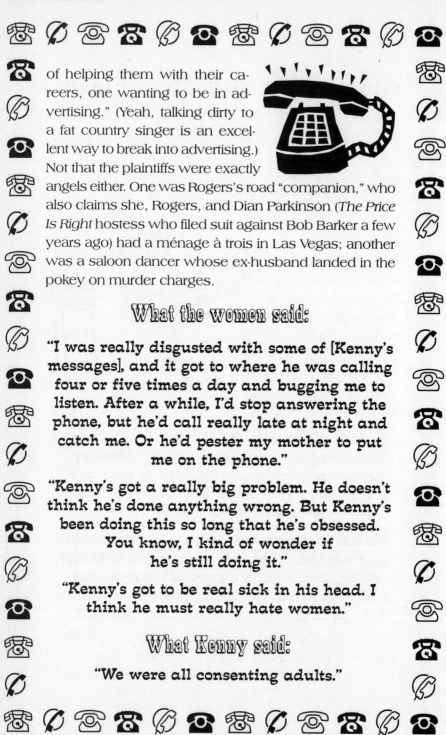

of helping them with their careers, one wanting to be in advertising." (Yeah, talking dirty to a fat country singer is an excellent way to break into advertising.) Not that the plaintiffs were exactly angels either. One was Rogers's road "companion," who also claims she, Rogers, and Dian Parkinson (*The Price Is Right* hostess who filed suit against Bob Barker a few years ago) had a ménage à trois in Las Vegas; another was a saloon dancer whose ex-husband landed in the pokey on murder charges.

What the women said:

"I was really disgusted with some of [Kenny's messages], and it got to where he was calling four or five times a day and bugging me to listen. After a while, I'd stop answering the phone, but he'd call really late at night and catch me. Or he'd pester my mother to put me on the phone."

"Kenny's got a really big problem. He doesn't think he's done anything wrong. But Kenny's been doing this so long that he's obsessed. You know, I kind of wonder if he's still doing it."

"Kenny's got to be real sick in his head. I think he must really hate women."

What Kenny said:

"We were all consenting adults."

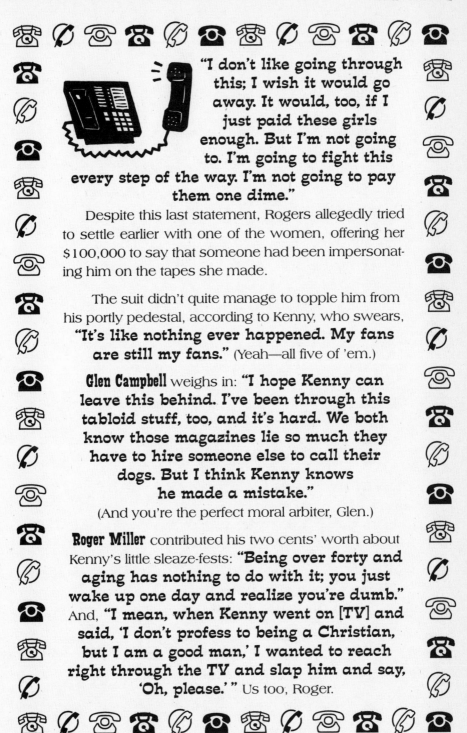

"I don't like going through this; I wish it would go away. It would, too, if I just paid these girls enough. But I'm not going to. I'm going to fight this every step of the way. I'm not going to pay them one dime."

Despite this last statement, Rogers allegedly tried to settle earlier with one of the women, offering her $100,000 to say that someone had been impersonating him on the tapes she made.

The suit didn't quite manage to topple him from his portly pedestal, according to Kenny, who swears, **"It's like nothing ever happened. My fans are still my fans."** (Yeah—all five of 'em.)

Glen Campbell weighs in: **"I hope Kenny can leave this behind. I've been through this tabloid stuff, too, and it's hard. We both know those magazines lie so much they have to hire someone else to call their dogs. But I think Kenny knows he made a mistake."**
(And you're the perfect moral arbiter, Glen.)

Roger Miller contributed his two cents' worth about Kenny's little sleaze-fests: **"Being over forty and aging has nothing to do with it; you just wake up one day and realize you're dumb."** And, **"I mean, when Kenny went on [TV] and said, 'I don't profess to being a Christian, but I am a good man,' I wanted to reach right through the TV and slap him and say, 'Oh, please.'"** Us too, Roger.

I Fall to Pieces

A World of Hurt

Sufferin' through major trauma seems to be a required part of being a hillbilly star—from life-threatening maladies to horrendous car crashes and heinous crimes—and may be part of what seasons a person into becoming the model of forbearance that truly defines the term "country singer."

Johnny Cash and his family were attacked in December 1981 at Cash's compound in Montego Bay, Jamaica. Three rough customers, all wearing bandannas and wielding hatchets and knives, robbed the country clan, making off with cash and jewelry to the tune of $50,000. (To add insult to injury, they made a clean getaway in **June Carter Cash**'s Land Rover.) **Tracy Lawrence** went through a similarly violent attack a little closer to home (in Nashville)—he was shot four times in a parking lot in the same week he'd put the finishing touches on his debut album, nearly ending his career before it began! Lawrence had accompanied good ol' galpal Sonja Wilkerson back to the motel where she was staying, and as they stepped out of the car, he says, "I turned around and was looking at the barrel of a gun." Lawrence and Wilkerson were robbed by a trio of desperadoes, who then demanded her room number. "In my mind," Lawrence recalled, "the only reason for taking us to a hotel room was to rape her. They didn't try to hide their faces. They would not have let us live. I decided that if I was going to die, I was going to die fighting." Lawrence grabbed for one man's gun—and immediately got shot by the bandido, whose bullet hit him in the finger. Then the other men opened fire, clipping him in the knee, hip, and shoulder. "The bullet in my hip missed a main artery by a tenth of a millimeter," he says. "The paramedics told me I would have bled to death in less than three minutes if it had hit my artery." Lucky Lawrence now carries a pistola with him wherever he goes.

Bill Anderson won a suit he filed against an allegedly drunk driver who plowed into Anderson's car and left his wife with permanent brain damage, and Boy Howdy's **Hugh Wright** was in a coma for five months after stopping to assist a stranded motorist and being hit himself by another car. Although he was later able to rejoin the band, the head injuries caused by the accident have left him with a permanent speech impediment. **Pam Tillis** nearly lost her life after drinking too much ("My major in college was music and partying") then getting behind the wheel and plowing into another car. The accident broke every bone in her face, and it took five years of surgery to put her together again.

Hank Williams, Jr. fell off a cliff during a hike in 1975, and landed smack dab onto a big boulder—on his face! Ouch! One witness said, "About the only thing he had left was the one eye. It literally tore his nose off, drove it up through his head and blew a hole in his forehead, which exposed the brain. And, as far as

Meet Indestructo-Man!

Trace Adkins has possibly faced more career-threatening injuries than anyone else in country today:

- ☀ Nearly lost his left leg when an oil tank exploded
- ☀ Nearly lost both legs after a heavy-equipment accident left him with severe cuts on his posterior
- ☀ Was seriously injured (punctured lungs, broken ribs, and torn-off nose, which was reattached by doctors) after driving his truck into a parked bus
- ☀ While working as an oilman, was trapped on top of an oil rig in the ocean during a hurricane ("I got to the highest part of the living quarters on the rig, so if it turned over, I was pretty well centered and could go in either direction.")
- ☀ Was shot by his first wife (see page 177)

But Trace's gravest injury came when his little finger was cut off as he attempted to open an oil container. Having been advised by his doctors that he wouldn't be able to move the damaged digit after they reattached it, Trace asked them to set it in a curl so that it would fit around a guitar neck.

A face that looks pretty decent—
considering all it's been through

the lower part of his head, his jaws, teeth, gums, they were pretty much ruined." Many, many operations and therapy sessions later, Williams was nearly normal again—at least physically.

Grave illnesses seem to be another hallmark of country stardom. **Johnny Cash**, initially thought to have Parkinson's disease, was diagnosed with the similarly symptomatic Shy-Drager Syndrome. **Donna Fargo** and **Clay Walker** have multiple sclerosis, and **Doug Stone** has suffered through several heart attacks (and continues to smoke!). And of course there's **Kevin Sharp**, who has cancer and is certainly not shy about sharing his pain with the world. From the pages of every magazine in which he's interviewed, he's seen grimacing in agony or confessing how thankful he is for having such a wonderful life after having gone through *so* much. (It's worth noting that Kevin was a member of the "Make a Wish" foundation—and for his wish, asked to meet legendary pop producer **David Foster** . . . some breaks are made, not born). A teevee movie of his tragic yet uplifting life story is in the works—yippee.

Hepatitis sufferers include **Kenny Rogers**, **Rodney Crowell**, and of course **Naomi Judd**—who talked about her illness on the pages of any women's magazine who would listen (pretty much all of them). Gazing from their covers, smiling tremulously, Naomi spouted quotes like, "I have never believed in complaining. . . . I've always been a brave little soldier," and, "I'm trying real hard to see it not as a tombstone but as a stepping stone."

We Must Have Been Out of Our Minds

> **"If you really want to try something unusual, try passin' out in front of five thousand people."**
> **(Loretta Lynn)**

Loretta Lynn is one of Music City's most famous cases of chronic illness. Beginning at a young age, Lynn was susceptible to migraines (she attempted suicide during a particularly bad one), depression, and every known illness in the annals of medicine (in 1972 alone, she landed in the hospital nine times!).

> **"I just pass out and go into a sort of coma, when I don't even know it's comin' on. . . . I think I'm one of the unhappiest people in the world."**
> **(Loretta Lynn)**

Loretta's incoherent patter, forgotten lyrics, and regular pass-outs on stage were so notorious that she was used as the model for the lead character in Robert Altman's *Nashville* (which Loretta's husband, Mooney, called "the worst goddamn movie I ever saw"). It can't all be chalked up to a frail constitution, however. Lynn admits that, "Every time I felt nervous, I took a pill. And at bedtime I had me still other pills to get to sleep."

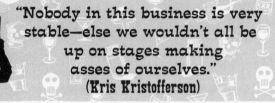

"Nobody in this business is very
stable—else we wouldn't all be
up on stages making
asses of ourselves."
(Kris Kristofferson)

Loretta's best girlfriend **Tammy Wynette** was
also ill—or thought she was—for most of her life,
enduring at least seventeen major surgeries, as
well as shock treatments ("They were horrible, but they helped me," she said) before
her death at age fifty-five in 1998. Like Loretta, during her various illnesses, Wynette
got hooked on "feel-good" pills. "They
tapered me off in the hospital, but
sometimes I had severe pain," she
said.

"Only Tammy Wynette and Alice Cooper
know how hard it is to be a woman."
(Alice Cooper)

Tammy used to "tell my children, 'I never took cocaine, marijuana or speed. I just took something to ease pain.' They blame me,
but they've never endured pain. They've never had operation one and
didn't know how to sympathize." According to Tammy, her kids "con-
demn me and make me feel like almost nothing. They have such strong
feelings, due to scars I left unintentionally. Never physical abuse, God
no. Only mental." Daughter Jackie Paule begs to differ. "The way I see
it, my mother had a goal — she wanted to be
an entertainer. And her family was second-
ary. She was gone all the time."

Perhaps the wildest inci-
dent in Ms. Wynette's colorful
existence was her purported ab-
duction at gunpoint in 1978.
She claimed that a stranger (the only thing she
really saw, she said, was "a brown glove, a lot
of hair on his arm, and two inches of gun

barrel") pointed a pistol at her in a Nashville parking lot, then made her drive to a secluded area far, far away where, she claimed, she was severely beaten. Wynette was found wandering around with a pair of pantyhose wound tightly around her neck. Rumors abounded about the incident (the culprit or culprits were never apprehended), and many on Music Row thought the incident a cheap hoax, staged for the publicity value it would bring the fading star. (Scoffs **George Jones**, "She refused to take a lie-detector test," and, "the whole affair was bullshit.")

> **"Where you lose it first is between the ears."**
> **(Conway Twitty)**

Jones himself is not exactly a model of stability. While he was drinking heavily, he says, "I took on two additional and dominant personalities. I even named them. One was 'Deedoodle the Duck,' and the other was the 'Old Man.' I quacked like the duck while speaking English, and I moaned like the old man, again in English. I went on for hours, and occasionally for days, unable to speak in my natural voice. . . . The duck sounded like Donald Duck and the old man something like Walter Brennan. They had personalities and passionate convictions of their own. Neither would take shit off the other." Jones once sang an entire show in his "duck" voice, an act so bizarre, even for George, that once again the men in white suits were called to cart him off to the loony bin.

A Fire I Can't Put Out

Some illnesses are a bit more suspect than others. One of the best explanations for a bout of bad behavior was given by **Charlie Rich's** reps after a notorious incident at the CMA Awards. When the Rich man, who was a presenter, opened the envelope for "Entertainer of the Year" and saw **John Denver's** name, he whipped out a lighter and set the paper ablaze. Later, his handlers said he'd been suffering the aftereffects of an insect bite. Try some Off! next time, Charlie!

Wasted Days and Wasted Nights

"If I knew I was going to live this long, I probably would have taken better care of myself."
(David Allan Coe)

Seems like the first thing someone does when they get famous is latch on to a drug or alcohol habit. Hotel rooms are trashed, marriages fall apart, bigger and better drugs are tried, more spectacular misbehavior occurs, and then finally the same thing happens to country stars that happens to rock stars and film stars and every other kind of star: They end up flat on their backs in mental wards or jail cells. Fortunately, they *can* get help—and, of course, boost their careers in the process when they brag about how they lived to tell it all. Sigh.

Hoyt Axton: marijuana

Was slapped with a $15,000 fine, a stint at community service, and a suspended prison sentence when cops found more than a pound of pot in his Montana abode. His wife, who was also charged (but given a suspended sentence), gave it to him to relieve pain he'd been suffering after he had a stroke. Oh, legalize it already!

Glen Campbell: booze, cocaine

"Alcohol was waiting to ambush me."

According to **Tanya Tucker**, when she first met Glen, alcohol had already ambushed him, judging from what happened when she and a girlfriend went to his hotel room after seeing one of his shows.

"Glen left the room for a while, and I remember wondering why. I didn't have to wonder for long, because when he walked back out in the living room he had nothing on but tennis shoes and socks. Not one stitch of clothes."

 "About 1978, I began to notice there was something wrong in the way some of the artists sounded in recording sessions. There was this nasal tone. It was like they were singing through their noses. I found out what the problem was—cocaine."
(**Rick Blackburn**, CBS executive)

Johnny Cash: booze, barbiturates, amphetamines, painkllers

Cash, long known for wrecking cars, trashing hotel rooms, missing shows, forgetting lyrics, and getting himself thrown into the hoosegow on a regular basis, was down to 140 pounds at one point, and almost died in 1967 from an overdose. He was also 86ed from the Grand Ole Opry after busting out some footlights in a drunken stupor.

"I crave amphetamines. Today, I'm not taking them, and I don't intend to take them tomorrow. But it's something that I can't help; it's my chemical makeup. The least little mood-altering thing that I might take, my system cries, 'Drugs, drugs, drugs! More, more, more!'"

"I didn't ever kick the drug habit, and I don't think I ever will. There will always be that gnawing."

"When I first met him, I was probably twelve or thirteen years old. He was just pilled to the gills, doped up and hyper and had all that nervous energy, but even still, he had that charm, that magic."
(**Dolly Parton**)

> **"I went to treatment with no intention of doing anything but getting out of jail."**
> **(Steve Earle)**

Rosanne Cash: cocaine

". . . one day you wake up and [your drug use is] not recreational anymore. It's the key emotional element in your life. And that's fuckin' scary."

Steve Earle: booze, heroin

"I knew toward the end that I was dying. I just didn't know if there was anything I could do about it. That's what addiction is."

Freddy Fender: booze, marijuana

"When I was sixteen, I dropped out of high school and joined the Marines. . . . I always liked to play the guitar in the barracks and to drink, so much so that sometimes I forgot where or who I was."

Larry Gatlin: cocaine

Hospitalized in December of 1984 for his cocaine addiction; decided to quit the day he found himself crawling around on a hotel room floor, picking up lint because it looked like coke, on which he was spending up to $10,000 per day!

Merle Haggard: marijuana, booze

> **"Booze was always easy to come by. Folks were always wanting to buy me a drink and they'd get mad if I turned them down. They didn't get mad very often."**
> **(George Jones)**

"There were wild times, good times, and times I don't remember too well."
(Merle Haggard)

Waylon Jennings: cocaine, booze, pills, marijuana

Used to room with **Johnny Cash** in an apartment, where they popped pills together and lived the swinging bachelor lifestyle. Jennings dropped to 135 pounds at one point, and was known for passing out in the middle of his songs. At the peak of his cocaine addiction, he was spending $1,500 a day on the drug.

**"I would snort half a gram in one side of my nose and half a gram in the other, shotgunning it. The tops of most people's heads would have come off if they did that."
(Waylon Jennings)**

**"[He] would swallow a doorknob if you offered him one."
(Carl Perkins)**

**"You really don't know who you are when you've spent twenty-one years on drugs."
(Waylon Jennings)**

**"... since he's quit drugs he's very boring. He's reliable and all that shit. He shows up, he sings good.
Who needs that."
(Willie Nelson)**

**"At this point, I've given up everything but oxygen."
(Waylon Jennings)**

George "No Show" Jones: booze, pills, cocaine

At one point, Jones was doing so much cocaine that he dropped to 100 pounds and had constantly bleeding gums.

In a delusional alcoholic stupor, Jones once drew a face on a pillow at home, shot it to smithereens, then called his buddies yelling, **"The king is dead! The king is dead!"**

"Amphetamines were very popular among Nashville musicians in the 1960s. One variety was yellow, and we called those pills 'old yellers.' Another was speckled, and we called those 'speckled birds.' Another was black, and we called those 'black beauties.' Another was nicknamed 'L.A. turnarounds.' The joke was that you could take one in Nashville, drive to Los Angeles, and turn around and drive back without sleep."

"Years later, when I missed hundreds of personal appearances because I was drunk, people around me tried to get me to lie. 'Tell the press you were sick, or that your sister was ill, or that your bus broke down,' they said. 'Hell no,' I said. 'Tell them I was drunk.' " Hey, wait—I thought it was that Mafia that done that to ya, George (see page 91).

"Shug [Baggott, Jr., his manager] got me started on it [cocaine] to keep me messed up, just the way he got me drunk all the time."

Ex-wife **Tammy Wynette** once thought she'd outsmart George by hiding the keys to every car, truck, and tractor on their spread so he couldn't get to the bars or liquor stores. **"But she forgot about the lawn mower,"** Jones says slyly. **"A key glistened in the ignition. I imagine the top speed for that old mower was five miles per hour. It might have taken an hour and a half or more for me to get to the liquor store, but get there I did."**

On cocaine: **"I even knew of people that were on it, like my good friend Waylon, who I was even trying to help from time to time. I tried it and it perked me up. They said I went onstage and did the best show I'd ever done, which I don't believe."**

Naomi Judd: marijuana

"I know now that dabbling in pot was just an immature diversion. It seemed like harmless recreation, just a plaything, and I took to it much like a child attaches itself to a bright shiny new toy. . . . I'm terribly ashamed and regretful now that I tried it."

"Never keep your pills and your
loose change in the same pocket—
because I just swallowed
thirty-five cents."
(Roger Miller)

Sammy Kershaw: cocaine, booze

"I was into drugs. I'm not talking about pot. I probably
smoked marijuana three times in my life. I didn't like it.
I snorted up Peru, though, you know?"

Hal Ketchum: booze, drugs

"I love opiates, and I had started developing some very
serious habits. I had turned to drugs and alcohol, and I
don't drink well—I've got too much Indian blood in me. It
ain't pretty. It ain't pretty at all. I just stayed stupid."

Kris Kristofferson: booze, drugs

Calls pot "laughing tobacco."

"I think I have all the chemistry to be a full-fledged
alcoholic or drug addict. I welcome oblivion like an old
friend sometimes."

Roger Miller: pills, booze

Used to throw down almost 100 pills per day; his drug and alcohol
problem got so bad that he had writer's block for five years.

Willie Nelson: marijuana, booze, pills

Once smoked a joint on the roof of the White House with an unnamed politico.

"I'm not in bad shape for a tequila-drinkin'
doper."
(Willie Nelson)

'Billies at Betty Ford

⊚ **Johnny Cash** (1984) for barbiturates, amphetamines, and painkillers. In 1989, made an additional stab at rehab in Tennessee.

⊚ **Mac Davis** ("The whiskey just started drinkin' me.")

⊚ **Hal Ketchum** ("I spent [a] Christmas in rehab.")

⊚ **Jerry Lee Lewis**

⊚ **Tanya Tucker** (1988)

⊚ **Tammy Wynette** (painkillers, 1986)

"We were swallowing enough pills to choke even Johnny Cash."

"The biggest killer on the planet is stress, and I still think the best medicine is and always has been cannabis. . . . I think most sensible human beings know it's not something you send people to the penitentiary for."

Hates coke: "If you're wired, you're fired."

". . . I suffer what the coach Darrell Royal calls the re-re's: the regrets and remorses. I'll sit on the side of the bed and think, 'Oh my god, did I really say that? Oh god, I didn't really tell them that shit, did I? Did I really get into a fighting disposition? Did I really start feeling very amorous at the same time I got too drunk to fuck? Oh god.' These are the re-re's."

Johnny Paycheck: booze, drugs

"Yes, I do cocaine, but cocaine isn't a killer drug and neither is alcohol. Cocaine and alcohol are okay, up-front drugs."

"Hell, I've been everywhere and done everything—twice. I've been up and down like a windowshade."

Johnny Rodriguez: cocaine, booze

Rodriguez was in and out of rehab most of his adult life—until he got nabbed for murder (see page 190).

"I pigged out on cocaine, and I paid. Cocaine was everywhere. I mean everywhere. Fans had it. My friends had it. Everybody was doing it—like beer back in Texas."

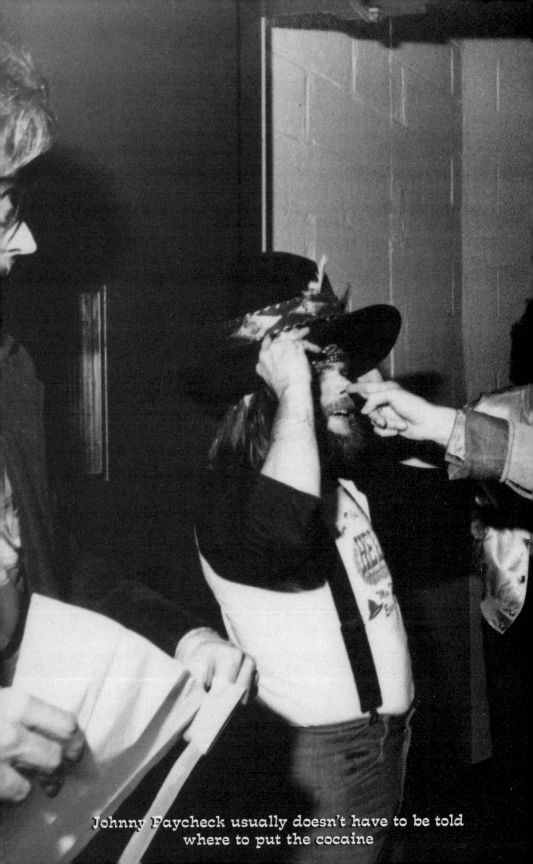

Johnny Paycheck usually doesn't have to be told
where to put the cocaine

They don't call 'im Kinky for nothin'

> **"I loved it, but I don't want anything
> to do with druggies."**
> **(Kenny Rogers**, whose drug experience, he says, is
> limited to a few puffs off a single solitary joint)

Ricky Van Shelton: booze

**"You go along and think you're just partyin' a little bit,
then one day it's got you, and you won't admit it to
yourself. Drinkin' about put me under the table."**

Merle Travis: pills

Had a hard time kicking barbiturates, and spent lots of time in
hospitals and mental institutions.

Randy Travis: various drugs, booze

**"I ran with people who used drugs,
people who sold. You can't believe
how many drugs there were ... and
how easy they were to get, and I did
anything I could get my hands on—
PCP, MDA, LSD, THC. I'm real
thankful that crack cocaine wasn't
around back then. Also, I was scared
of needles. That and not having
crack probably saved me from complete
self-destruction."**

Cleaned up his act after meeting hillbilly hag Lib Hatcher.

Travis Tritt: booze, pills

**"I did get caught up in that trap for a while. Drinking
real heavy. And doing those little pills to keep me awake
and going. It's hard not to."**

Tanya Tucker: booze, cocaine

**"Going through rehab, you sit there and
hear about other people and their life
stories, how unloved they were. .... I just
wanted to have a good time."**

**"It's very hard to have thousands of people scream-
ing for you and then go back to a hotel room alone.
I think that's why I'm always looking for a party
after the show."**

Tucker once ordered a drink at a club in New York, then
leaped the bar and asked the male
barkeep if she could pay him by
putting the money in his pants.

At an Epic Records industry
party in 1997, Tucker had a
couple of drinks (with TV journalist
Stone Phillips, who was doing a story on her, in tow).
After shouting back and forth with **Ty Herndon**, who was
onstage performing at the time, she lifted her shirt and
flashed the entire place—and was asked to leave.
**"Actually it was very hot and I lifted up my
sweater to get some air in there. I didn't
think people would make such a big deal out of it."**

Shania Twain: nada

**"I probably looked high. I used to really rock out. I'd get
people coming up to me saying, 'Do you do drugs or
what?' I never did, but I looked like I did."**

Keith Whitley: booze

Died May 9, 1989 of an alcohol overdose; found with a blood alcohol level of .477. Trust us—that's a lot.

Hank Williams: booze, pills

Used to use the TV sets and walls in his hotel
rooms for target practice, and once shot at
his wife and a couple of her friends in a
drunken rage.

Died of an overdose before he was thirty;
in his bloodstream were morphine, chloral
hydrate, and alcohol. A cop said, **"[At the
Andrew Jackson Hotel] he was**

lifeless as they put his clothes on him. The porters carried him out and put him on the backseat of the car. Williams never moved at all. He seemed to make a coughing-like sound (only twice) as they carried [him], but was lifeless and didn't move. . . .

After investigating this matter, I think that Williams was dead when he was dressed and carried out of the hotel. . . . A man drunk or doped will make some movement if you move them. A dead man will make a coughing sound if they are lifted around."

Hank Williams, Jr.: booze, pills, cocaine

"I'd just put Daddy's record on the jukebox and get a nice fifth of whiskey and a couple of downers and sit there and try to communicate with him."

In the throes of his addiction, Williams attempted suicide and had a nervous breakdown, was hospitalized many times for drug overdoses, and lost a ton of money in settlements with club owners who sued him for being a no-show.

"Sex feels good, Jim Beam tastes good, but cocaine will kill your ass."

Tammy Wynette: pills

"When you're bent over double and have to perform in front of thousands of people, you have to take something to relieve it."

Faron Young: booze, pills

Son Robyn said his dad was

"painful to be around."

I Dreamed of a Hillbilly Heaven

"No matter how big you get, the size of your funeral depends on the weather."
(Roger Miller)

Tragic fatalities in the country pantheon

Joe Carson: car accident (February 1964)

Patsy Cline: airplane crash (March 1963)
"The last thing I said to Patsy was, 'I'm really going to be worried about you flying in this weather.' She said, 'Don't worry about me. When it's my time to go, it's my time.'"
(Dottie West)

Johnny Horton: car accident
Horton's car was struck by a drunk nineteen-year-old in Texas. Everyone involved in the accident survived except Horton. (Eerie Hank connection: Horton had just played Austin's Skyline, the last place Hank played . . . and Horton's widow, Billie Jean, had also been married to Hank.)

Ira Louvin (half of the legendary Louvin Brothers): 1965, head-on collision with a drunk driver in Missouri. Everyone died.

Seven out of nine members of **Reba McEntire**'s band, plus her tour manager, died in a horrible plane crash (it plowed into a mountain) near San Diego in 1991. Reba was supposed to have been on the plane herself, but she had decided to stay in town to get some rest and fly out the next day.

Jimmie Osborne: suicide (1957)

Jim Reeves: plane crash (1964)

> "Once you're [dead], you're beloved. You
> know, 'the late, great,' and 'what he did for
> our music.' But until then it's always
> 'troublemakin' son of a bitch.'"
> **(Waylon Jennings)**

Steve Sanders (Oak Ridge Boys): shot himself at his home in Cape
Coral, Florida, in 1998

Mel Street: suicide (1978)

> "I later learned that Mel had eaten breakfast, chatted
> with his family, casually climbed the stairs to his bed-
> room, put a gun to his head, and pulled the trigger. He
> committed suicide on his forty-fifth birthday, as did his
> father, as did his grandfather. . . ."
> **(George Jones)**

Stringbean (David Akeman) and wife
Estelle: murdered (1973)

Local good-for-nothings John and
Doug Brown, having heard that
String didn't believe in banks and
had hidden a large sum somewhere in his home, broke into the
place during one of his Grand Ole
Opry appearances. Not having any
success at locating the stash, they
waited inside the house, listening
to his performance on the radio.
When String and his wife returned
home, the Browns accosted them
and demanded money. When
String refused to cough up, they
shot him dead—then blasted
Estelle as she attempted to flee.
The murderers got away with
$250 in cash, one of String's stage
costumes, an electric chainsaw,
and a couple of guns. They were

Alive and Pickin'

The plane crash that took the lives of
Buddy Holly, Ritchie Valens,
and the **Big Bopper** nearly claimed
Waylon Jennings's life as well.
Waylon, who was Holly's guitarist at the
time, says, "I have a terrible guilt about
that. . . . when I gave up my seat on the
plane to the Big Bopper, Buddy came
over to me and said, 'Well, you're not
going to go on the plane tonight?' And I
said, 'No. Bopper wanted to go.' So he
says, 'Well, I hope your old bus freezes
up.' And I shot back, 'Well, I hope your
plane crashes!' Imagine how I felt. I was
just twenty years old, and I thought I'd
caused the accident. It took me two
years to get over that before I could get
back to making music."

apprehended a few months later, convicted, and given consecutive ninety-nine-year sentences in prison. (In a bizarre footnote to the crime, the house's current owner recently found the money the men had been looking for—$20,000 in rat-nibbled bills in the fireplace.)

Jud Strunk: plane crash (1981)

Dottie West: car accident (September 1991)

Due for a performance at the Grand Ole Opry, she found herself stranded at home when her car wouldn't start. She was offered a ride by her elderly (eighty years old) neighbor, and they had almost made it to the Opry when he lost control of the car and crashed. Though West was rushed to the hospital, she later died from her injuries.

Faron Young: suicide (December 1996)

Young was found in his bed with a self-inflicted gunshot wound to the temple. He'd been having medical problems, including prostate trouble and emphysema.

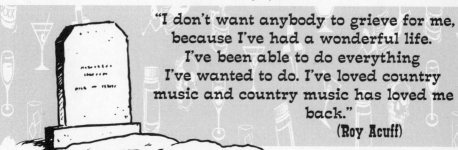

"I don't want anybody to grieve for me, because I've had a wonderful life. I've been able to do everything I've wanted to do. I've loved country music and country music has loved me back."
(Roy Acuff)

When the Grass Grows Over Me
"AND THE $HIT TOP HERE."
(Sammy Kershaw, on his desired tombstone inscription)

COUNTRY PLATINUM

Who's gone platinum? (And no, we don't mean from a bottle of hair-dye.) The Recording Industry Association of America certifies platinum status for an album once it has surpassed one million copies sold (records are certified gold when they've sold half that quantity). Following are the country stars and albums that have made it to this coveted mark; multiple-platinum albums are denoted with multiple LP icons to the left of the title (e.g., if an album is triple platinum, you'll see three LPs to the left of its title).

Trace Adkins
- Dreamin' Out Loud

Alabama
- 40 Hour Week
- Alabama Christmas
- Alabama Live
- American Pride
- Cheap Seats
- The Closer You Get
- Feels So Right
- For the Record: 41 Number One Hits
- Greatest Hits
- Greatest Hits, Volume II
- Greatest Hits, Volume III
- In Pictures
- Mountain Music
- My Home's in Alabama
- Pass It on Down
- Roll On
- Southern Star
- The Touch

John Anderson
- Seminole Wind

Lynn Anderson
- Rose Garden

Eddy Arnold
- Welcome to My World

David Ball
- Thinkin' Problem

The Bellamy Brothers
- Greatest Hits

John Berry
- John Berry

Clint Black
- The Greatest Hits
- The Hard Way
- Killin' Time
- No Time to Kill
- One Emotion
- Put Yourself in My Shoes

BlackHawk
- BlackHawk

Suzy Bogguss
- Aces

Brooks & Dunn
⦿⦿ *Borderline*
⦿⦿⦿⦿⦿ *Brand New Man*
⦿⦿ *The Greatest Hits Collection*
⦿⦿⦿⦿ *Hard Workin' Man*
⦿ *If You See Her*
⦿⦿⦿ *Waitin' on Sundown*

Garth Brooks
⦿⦿⦿ *Beyond the Season*
⦿⦿⦿⦿⦿⦿⦿ *The Chase*
⦿⦿⦿⦿⦿⦿⦿⦿⦿⦿⦿⦿⦿ *Double Live*
⦿⦿⦿⦿⦿⦿ *Fresh Horses*
⦿⦿⦿⦿⦿⦿⦿⦿ *Garth Brooks*
⦿⦿⦿ *The Garth Brooks Collection*
⦿⦿⦿⦿⦿⦿⦿⦿⦿ *The Hits*
⦿⦿⦿⦿⦿⦿⦿⦿ *In Pieces*
⦿⦿⦿⦿⦿⦿⦿⦿⦿⦿⦿⦿⦿⦿⦿⦿ *No Fences*
⦿⦿⦿⦿⦿⦿⦿⦿⦿⦿⦿⦿⦿⦿ *Ropin' the Wind*
⦿⦿⦿⦿⦿⦿ *Sevens*

Tracy Byrd
⦿⦿ *No Ordinary Man*

Glen Campbell
⦿ *By the Time I Get to Phoenix*
⦿ *Greatest Hits*
⦿⦿ *Wichita Lineman*

Mary Chapin Carpenter
⦿⦿⦿ *Come On, Come On*
⦿ *Shooting Straight in the Dark*
⦿ *Stones in the Road*

Deana Carter
⦿⦿⦿⦿ *Did I Shave My Legs for This?*

Johnny Cash
⦿⦿ *Greatest Hits*
⦿⦿ *Johnny Cash at Folsom Prison*
⦿⦿ *Johnny Cash at San Quentin*
⦿ *The Johnny Cash Portrait*

Mark Chesnutt
⦿ *Almost Goodbye*
⦿ *Longnecks and Short Stories*
⦿ *Too Cold at Home*

Terri Clark
⦿ *Terri Clark*

Patsy Cline
⦿⦿⦿⦿⦿⦿⦿ *Greatest Hits*
⦿ *The Patsy Cline Story*

David Allan Coe
⦿ *Greatest Hits*

Confederate Railroad
⦿ *Confederate Railroad*
⦿ *Notorious*

Rita Coolidge
⦿ *Anytime . . . Anywhere*

Billy Ray Cyrus
⦿ *It Won't Be the Last*
⦿⦿⦿⦿⦿⦿⦿⦿ *Some Gave All*

Mac Davis
⦿ *Baby, Don't Get Hooked on Me*

Diamond Rio
⦿ *Diamond Rio*
⦿ *Love a Little Stronger*

Joe Diffie
- Honky Tonk Attitude
- Third Rock from the Sun

The Dixie Chicks
- ●●●● Wide Open Spaces

Tennessee Ernie Ford
- Hymns
- The Star Carol

Jeff Foxworthy
- Crank It Up: The Music Album
- ●●● Games Rednecks Play
- ●●● You Might Be a Redneck If . . .

Larry Gatlin
- Straight Ahead

Crystal Gayle
- We Must Believe in Magic
- When I Dream

Vince Gill
- Best of Vince Gill
- High Lonesome Sound
- ●●●● I Still Believe in You
- ●● Let There Be Peace on Earth
- ●● Pocket Full of Gold
- ●● Souvenirs
- ●● When I Call Your Name
- ●●●● When Love Finds You

Amy Grant
- Age to Age
- A Christmas Album
- The Collection
- ●●●●● Heart in Motion
- ●●● Home for Christmas
- House of Love
- Unguarded

Lee Greenwood
- Greatest Hits

Merle Haggard
- The Best of the Best of Merle Haggard
- His Epic Hits—The First Eleven—To Be Continued
- Okie from Muskogee

Merle Haggard and **Willie Nelson**
- Poncho & Lefty

Faith Hill
- ●● Faith
- ●●● It Matters to Me
- ●● Take Me As I Am
- ●"This Kiss" (single)

Johnny Horton
- Johnny Horton's Greatest Hits

Alan Jackson
- ●●●● Don't Rock the Jukebox
- ●● Everything I Love
- ●●●● The Greatest Hits Collection
- ●● Here in the Real World
- High Mileage
- Honky Tonk Christmas
- ●●●●●● A Lot About Livin' (And a Little 'Bout Love)
- ●●●● Who I Am

Waylon Jennings
- ●●●● Greatest Hits
- Ol' Waylon

Jennings/Colter/Nelson/Glaser
- ●● The Outlaws

229

George Jones
- I Am What I Am
- Super Hits

The Judds
- Christmas Time with the Judds
- ◉◉ Greatest Hits
- Heartland
- Love Can Build a Bridge
- Rockin' with the Rhythm
- ◉◉ Why Not Me

Toby Keith
- Toby Keith
- Toby Keith Greatest Hits, Volume 1

The Kentucky Headhunters
- ◉◉ Pickin' on Nashville

Sammy Kershaw
- Don't Go Near the Water
- Haunted Heart

Alison Krauss
- ◉◉ Now That I've Found You

Tracy Lawrence
- ◉◉ Alibis
- I See It Now
- Sticks and Stones
- Time Marches On

Little Texas
- ◉◉ Big Time
- Kick a Little

Patty Loveless
- Honky Tonk Angel
- Only What I Feel
- When Fallen Angels Fly

Kathy Mattea
- A Collection of Hits

The Mavericks
- What a Crying Shame

Martina McBride
- Evolution
- The Way That I Am
- Wild Angels

Neal McCoy
- No Doubt About It
- You Gotta Love That!

Mindy McCready
- Ten Thousand Angels

Reba McEntire
- ◉◉◉ For My Broken Heart
- ◉◉◉ Greatest Hits
- ◉◉◉◉◉ Greatest Hits, Volume II
- ◉◉◉ It's Your Call
- The Last One to Know
- ◉◉ Merry Christmas to You
- ◉◉◉ Read My Mind
- Reba
- Reba Live
- ◉◉◉ Rumor Has It
- Starting Over
- Sweet Sixteen
- What If It's You
- Whoever's in New England

Tim McGraw
- ◉◉ All I Want
- ◉◉◉ Everywhere
- ◉◉◉◉◉ Not a Moment Too Soon

Ronnie Milsap
- ◉◉ Greatest Hits
- Greatest Hits, Volume II

John Michael Montgomery

- ⦿⦿⦿⦿ *John Michael Montgomery*
- ⦿⦿⦿⦿ *Kickin' It Up*
- ⦿⦿⦿ *Life's a Dance*

Lorrie Morgan

- ⦿ *Greatest Hits*
- ⦿ *Leave the Light On*
- ⦿ *Something in Red*
- ⦿ *Watch Me*

Anne Murray

- ⦿⦿ *Christmas Wishes*
- ⦿⦿⦿⦿ *Greatest Hits*
- ⦿ *Let's Keep It That Way*
- ⦿ *New Kind of Feeling*

Willie Nelson

- ⦿⦿⦿⦿ *Always on My Mind*
- ⦿ *City of New Orleans*
- ⦿⦿ *Honeysuckle Rose soundtrack*
- ⦿ *Pretty Paper*
- ⦿⦿ *Red Headed Stranger*
- ⦿ *Somewhere Over the Rainbow*
- ⦿⦿⦿⦿ *Stardust*
- ⦿⦿⦿⦿ *Willie and Family Live*
- ⦿ *Willie Nelson Sings Kristofferson*
- ⦿⦿⦿ *Willie Nelson's Greatest Hits (& Some That Will Be)*
- ⦿ *Without a Song*

Willie Nelson and Waylon Jennings

- ⦿⦿ *Waylon & Willie*

Juice Newton

- ⦿ *Juice*

The Nitty Gritty Dirt Band

- ⦿ *Will the Circle Be Unbroken, Volumes 1 & 2*

The Oak Ridge Boys

- ⦿⦿ *Fancy Free*
- ⦿⦿ *Greatest Hits*

K. T. Oslin

- ⦿ *80's Ladies*
- ⦿ *This Woman*

Dolly Parton

- ⦿ *Eagle When She Flies*
- ⦿ *Greatest Hits*
- ⦿ *Here You Come Again*
- ⦿ *Slow Dancing with the Moon*

Dolly Parton, Linda Ronstadt, Emmylou Harris

- ⦿ *Trio*

Johnny Paycheck

- ⦿ *Take This Job and Shove It*

Eddie Rabbitt

- ⦿ *Horizon*

Collin Raye

- ⦿ *All I Can Be*
- ⦿ *The Best of Collin Raye: Direct Hits*
- ⦿ *Extremes*
- ⦿ *I Think About You*
- ⦿ *In This Life*

Charlie Rich

- ⦿ *Behind Closed Doors*

LeAnn Rimes

- ○○○○○○ Blue
- ○ Sittin' on Top of the World
- ○○ Unchained Melody: The Early Years
- ○○○○ You Light Up My Life: Inspirational Songs

Marty Robbins

- ○ Gunfighter Ballads & Trail Songs

Kenny Rogers

- ○ 20 Great Years
- ○○○○ 20 Greatest Hits
- ○ Best of Kenny Rogers and the First Edition
- ○○ Christmas
- ○ Daytime Friends
- ○ Duets (With Kim Carnes, Dottie West, Sheena Easton)
- ○○ Eyes That See in the Dark
- ○○○○○ The Gambler
- ○ Gideon
- ○○○○○○○○○○○○ Greatest Hits
- ○○○ Kenny
- ○ Kenny Rogers
- ○ Love Will Turn You Around
- ○ Share Your Love
- ○○○○ Ten Years of Gold
- ○ We've Got Tonight
- ○ What About Me?

Kenny Rogers and Dolly Parton

- ○○ Once Upon a Christmas

Kenny Rogers and Dottie West

- ○ Classics

Dan Seals

- ○ The Best of Dan Seals

Ricky Van Shelton

- ○ Backroads
- ○ Greatest Hits Plus
- ○ Loving Proof
- ○ RVS III
- ○ Wild-Eyed Dream

Ricky Skaggs

- ○ Highways and Heartaches

The Statler Brothers

- ○○○ Best of the Statler Brothers
- ○ Christmas Card

Ray Stevens

- ○ Greatest Hits
- ○ He Thinks He's Ray Stevens

Doug Stone

- ○ Doug Stone
- ○ I Thought It Was You

George Strait

- ○ #7
- ○ Beyond the Blue Neon
- ○○ Blue Clear Sky
- ○○○ Carrying Your Love with Me
- ○ The Chill of an Early Fall
- ○ Does Fort Worth Ever Cross Your Mind
- ○○ Easy Come, Easy Go
- ○ George Strait—Live!
- ○○○ Greatest Hits
- ○○○ Greatest Hits, Volume II
- ○ Holding My Own

George Strait, continued
- ○ *If You Ain't Lovin' (You Ain't Livin')*
- ○○ *Lead On*
- ○ *Livin' It Up*
- ○○ *Merry Christmas Strait to You*
- ○○ *Ocean Front Property*
- ○ *One Step at a Time*
- ○○○○○ *Pure Country*
- ○ *Right or Wrong*
- ○ *Something Special*
- ○ *Strait Country*
- ○ *Strait from the Heart*
- ○○○○○○ *Strait Out of the Box*
- ○ *Ten Strait Hits*

Pam Tillis
- ○ *Homeward Looking Angel*
- ○ *Sweetheart's Dance*

Aaron Tippin
- ○ *Read Between the Lines*

The Tractors
- ○○ *The Tractors*

Randy Travis
- ○○○○○ *Always & Forever*
- ○ *Greatest Hits, Volume I*
- ○ *Greatest Hits, Volume II*
- ○ *Heroes & Friends*
- ○ *High Lonesome*
- ○○ *No Holdin' Back*
- ○○ *Old 8x10*
- ○○○ *Storms of Life*

Travis Tritt
- ○○ *Country Club*
- ○ *Greatest Hits—From the Beginning*
- ○○○ *It's All About to Change*
- ○ *The Restless Kind*
- ○○ *Ten Feet Tall and Bulletproof*
- ○○ *T-R-O-U-B-L-E*

Tanya Tucker
- ○ *Can't Run from Yourself*
- ○ *Greatest Hits 1990–1992*
- ○ *What Do I Do With Me*

Shania Twain
- ○○○○○○○○○ *Come on Over*
- ○○○○○○○○○○ *The Woman in Me*

Conway Twitty
- ○ *The Very Best of Conway Twitty*

Clay Walker
- ○ *Clay Walker*
- ○ *Hypnotize the Moon*
- ○ *If I Could Make a Living*
- ○ *Rumor Has It*

Keith Whitley
- ○ *Greatest Hits*

Hank Williams
- ○ *24 of Hank Williams' Greatest Hits*
- ○ *40 Greatest Hits*

Hank Williams, Jr.

- Born to Boogie
- Greatest Hits, Volume I
- Greatest Hits, Volume II
- Greatest Hits, Volume III
- Hank Live
- Hank Williams, Jr.'s Greatest Hits
- Major Moves
- The Pressure Is On
- The Very Best of Hank Williams
- Whiskey Bent & Hell Bound

Tammy Wynette

- Greatest Hits

Wynonna

- Revelations
- Tell Me Why
- Wynonna

Trisha Yearwood

- Hearts in Armor
- The Song Remembers When
- Songbook: A Collection of Hits
- Thinkin' About You
- Trisha Yearwood

Dwight Yoakam

- Buenas Noches from a Lonely Room
- Guitars, Cadillacs, Etc., Etc.
- Hillbilly Deluxe
- If There Was a Way
- Just Lookin' for a Hit
- This Time

WHERE Y'ALL FROM?

Washington

Lila McCann
Mark O'Connor

Montana

Nicolette Larson

California

Gary Allan
Skip Ewing
Lee Greenwood
Merle Haggard
John McEuen
Kevin Sharp
Cliffie Stone

WHERE Y'ALL FROM?

Oklahoma

Hoyt Axton
Joe Diffie
Wade Hayes
Reba McEntire
Floyd Tillman

Garth Brooks
Ty England
Toby Keith
Jean Shepard
Bryan White

Jeff Carson
Vince Gill
Susie Luchsinger
B. J. Thomas
Sheb Wooley

Arizona

Michael Peterson

Texas

Gene Autry
Junior Brown
Tracy Byrd
Mark Chesnutt
Rodney Crowell
Ronnie Dunn
Holly Dunn
Joe Ely
Freddy Fender
Radney Foster
Jimmy Dale Gilmore
Johnny Gimble
Nancy Griffith
Tish Hinojosa

Waylon Jennings
George Jones
David Kersh
Kris Kristofferson
Johnny Lee
Lyle Lovett
Barbara Mandrell
Irlene Mandrell
Louise Mandrell
Delbert McClinton
Neal McCoy
Gary Morris
Michael Martin Murphey
Willie Nelson
Buck Owens
Lee Roy Parnell

Ray Price
Ronna Reeves
Johnny Rodriguez
Kenny Rogers
Dan Seals
Jason Sellers
Billy Joe Shaver
George Strait
Doug Supernaw
Hank Thompson
Tanya Tucker
Clay Walker
Gene Watson
Don Williams
Lee Ann Womack

Mississippi

Steve Azar
Moe Bandy
Jerry Clower
Faith Hill
Chris LeDoux
Paul Overstreet
Charley Pride
LeAnn Rimes
Marty Stuart
Tammy Wynette

Alabama

Razzy Bailey
Vern Gosdin
Emmylou Harris
Ty Herndon
Charlie Louvin
Mac McAnally
Jeanne Pruett

Georgia

Rhett Akins
T. Graham Brown
Roy Drusky
Jeff Foxworthy
Alan Jackson
Cledus T. Judd
Brenda Lee
Billy Joe Royal
Ray Stevens
Doug Stone
Travis Tritt
Trisha Yearwood

Louisiana

Trace Adkins
Kix Brooks
Floyd Cramer
Mickey Gilley
Sammy Kershaw
Tim McGraw
Eddy Raven
Jo-El Sonnier
Hank Williams, Jr.

Florida

John Anderson
James Bonamy
Billy Dean
Hank Locklin
The Mavericks
Mindy McCready
Mel Tillis
Pam Tillis
Aaron Tippin
Slim Whitman

N
W E
S

WHERE Y'ALL FROM?

Tennessee

Deborah Allen	Deana Carter
Eddy Arnold	Rosanne Cash
Chet Atkins	Kenny Chesney
Mandy Barnett	Mark Collie
Matraca Berg	Ralph Emery
Owen Bradley	Ronnie McDowell
Kippi Brannon	Lorrie Morgan
Carlene Carter	Dolly Parton
	T. G. Sheppard
	Kitty Wells

North Carolina

Billy "Crash" Craddock
Charlie Daniels
Donna Fargo
Don Gibson
George Hamilton IV
Ronnie Milsap
Del Reeves
Earl Scruggs
Randy Travis

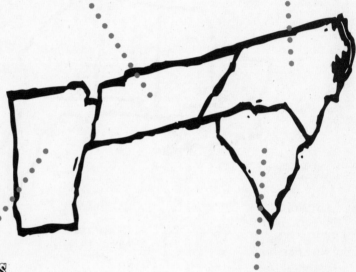

Arkansas

Jim Ed Brown
Glen Campbell
Johnny Cash
David Frizzell
Royal Wade Kimes
Tracy Lawrence
K.T. Oslin
Collin Raye

South Carolina

Bill Anderson
David Ball
John Berry

North Dakota

Lynn Anderson

Wisconsin

Felice Bryant
Pee Wee King

Ohio

Bobby Bare
David Allan Coe
Earl Thomas Conley
Johnny Paycheck
Roy Rogers
Shelly West

Indiana

Janie Fricke
Connie Smith
Steve Wariner

Kansas

Martina McBride

Missouri

Helen Cornelius
Sara Evans
Rich McCready
Porter Wagoner
Chely Wright

Illinois

Suzy Bogguss
Alison Krauss
David Lee Murphy

Massachusetts
Jo Dee Messina

New York
Hal Ketchum
Eddie Rabbitt
Jerry Jeff Walker

Pennsylvania
Lacy J. Dalton
The Kinleys
Jeannie Seely

West Virginia
Asleep at the Wheel
Little Jimmy Dickens
Kathy Mattea

New Jersey
Clint Black
Mary Chapin Carpenter
Don Edwards

Virginia
June Carter Cash
Roy Clark
Steve Earle
Shelby Lynne
Juice Newton
Ricky Van Shelton

Kentucky
John Conlee
Billy Ray Cyrus
Skeeter Davis
Crystal Gayle
Tom T. Hall
Harlan Howard
Grandpa Jones
Naomi & Wynonna Judd
Patty Loveless
Loretta Lynn
Mila Mason
John Michael Montgomery
Ricky Skaggs
Dwight Yoakam

INDEX

J

K

O

P

Paglia, Camille . . . 58
Parkinson, Dian . . . 198
Parnell, Lee Roy . . . 18, 29,
    86, 87, 236
Parton, Dolly . . . 10, 18, 31,
    41, 45, 52, 53, 60, 66,
    69, 98, 112, 113, 125,
    134, 135, 140, 172, 173,
    211, 231, 232, 238
Paule, Jackie . . . 208
Paycheck, Johnny . . . 59, 65,
    71, 86, 96, 138, 189,
    190, 195, 217, 218, 231,
    239
Pearl, Minnie . . . 29
Perkins, Carl . . . 214
Peterson, Michael . . . 236
Phillips, Stone . . . 221
Pierce, Webb . . . 86, 129,
    130
Presley, Elvis . . . 104, 130
Price, Ray . . . 86, 87, 236
Pride, Charley . . . 5, 29, 237
Pruett, Jeanne . . . 237

R

Rabbitt, Eddie . . . 21, 63, 87,
    231, 240
Randall, Jon . . . 148
Raven, Eddy . . . 237
Raye, Collin . . . 29, 66, 102,
    138, 231, 238
Reagan, Ronald . . . 186
Reeves, Del . . . 85, 238
Reeves, Jim . . . 223
Reeves, Ronna . . . 236
Reynolds, Burt . . . 149

Reynolds, Robert . . . 109,
    148
Rich, Charlie . . . 65, 209,
    231
Richie, Lionel . . . 68
Ricochet . . . 90, 146
Riley, Jeannie C. . . . 79
Rimes, LeAnn . . . 3, 17, 18,
    22, 58, 71, 83, 106, 136,
    137, 195, 232, 237
Robbins, Marty . . . 79, 232
Roberts, Julia . . . 53
Rodgers, Jimmie . . . 31
Rodman, Dennis . . . 68
Rodriguez, Johnny . . . 21,
    138, 147, 190, 191, 217,
    236
Roe, Marty . . . 22, 131
Rogers, Kenny . . . 9, 47, 48,
    54, 87, 129, 134, 147,
    148, 149, 166, 172, 196,
    197, 198, 199, 206, 220,
    232, 236
Rogers, Roy . . . 59, 186, 239
Ronstadt, Linda . . . 231
Rourke, Mickey . . . 135
Royal, Billy Joe . . . 25, 86,
    237
Ruth, Jack . . . 12

S

Sams, Dean . . . 22
Sanders, Janet Anne . . . 181
Sanders, Steve . . . 123, 181,
    224
Sawyer Brown . . . 22
Schneider, John . . . 64
Schwarzenegger, Arnold . . .
    138